INTRODUCING
ISSUES WITH
OPPOSING
VIEWPOINTS®

Synthetic Drugs

Mary E. Williams, *Book Editor*

GREENHAVEN PRESS

A part of Gale, Cengage Learning

GALE
CENGAGE Learning·

Farmington Hills, Mich • San Francisco • New York • Waterville, Maine
Meriden, Conn • Mason, Ohio • Chicago

Elizabeth Des Chenes, *Director, Content Strategy*
Douglas Dentino, *Manager, New Product*

LIBRARY OF CONGRESS CATALOGING-IN-PUBLICATION DATA

Synthetic drugs / Mary E. Williams, book editor.
    pages cm. -- (Introducing issues with opposing viewpoints)
  Includes bibliographical references and index.
  ISBN 978-0-7377-6929-6 (hardcover)
  1. Synthetic drugs--Juvenile literature. 2. Drug abuse--Juvenile literature. I. Williams, Mary E., 1960-
  HV5809.5.S96 2014
  362.29'9--dc23
                                                              2013047325

Printed in the United States of America
1 2 3 4 5 6 7 18 17 16 15 14

Contents

Chapter 3: What Is the Best Way to Prevent Synthetic Drug Abuse?

Foreword

I ndulging in a wide spectrum of ideas, beliefs, and perspectives is a critical cornerstone of democracy. After all, it is often debates over differences of opinion, such as whether to legalize abortion, how to treat prisoners, or when to enact the death penalty, that shape our society and drive it forward. Such diversity of thought is frequently regarded as the hallmark of a healthy and civilized culture. As the Reverend Clifford Schutjer of the First Congregational Church in Mansfield, Ohio, declared in a 2001 sermon, "Surrounding oneself with only like-minded people, restricting what we listen to or read only to what we find agreeable is irresponsible. Refusing to entertain doubts once we make up our minds is a subtle but deadly form of arrogance." With this advice in mind, Introducing Issues with Opposing Viewpoints books aim to open readers' minds to the critically divergent views that comprise our world's most important debates.

Introducing Issues with Opposing Viewpoints simplifies for students the enormous and often overwhelming mass of material now available via print and electronic media. Collected in every volume is an array of opinions that captures the essence of a particular controversy or topic. Introducing Issues with Opposing Viewpoints books embody the spirit of nineteenth-century journalist Charles A. Dana's axiom: "Fight for your opinions, but do not believe that they contain the whole truth, or the only truth." Absorbing such contrasting opinions teaches students to analyze the strength of an argument and compare it to its opposition. From this process readers can inform and strengthen their own opinions, or be exposed to new information that will change their minds. Introducing Issues with Opposing Viewpoints is a mosaic of different voices. The authors are statesmen, pundits, academics, journalists, corporations, and ordinary people who have felt compelled to share their experiences and ideas in a public forum. Their words have been collected from newspapers, journals, books, speeches, interviews, and the Internet, the fastest growing body of opinionated material in the world.

Introducing Issues with Opposing Viewpoints shares many of the well-known features of its critically acclaimed parent series, Opposing Viewpoints. The articles are presented in a pro/con format, allowing readers to absorb divergent perspectives side by side. Active reading questions preface each viewpoint, requiring the student to approach the material thoughtfully and carefully. Useful charts, graphs, and cartoons supplement each article. A thorough introduction provides readers with crucial background on an issue. An annotated bibliography points the reader toward articles, books, and websites that contain additional information on the topic. An appendix of organizations to contact contains a wide variety of charities, nonprofit organizations, political groups, and private enterprises that each hold a position on the issue at hand. Finally, a comprehensive index allows readers to locate content quickly and efficiently.

Introducing Issues with Opposing Viewpoints is also significantly different from Opposing Viewpoints. As the series title implies, its presentation will help introduce students to the concept of opposing viewpoints and learn to use this material to aid in critical writing and debate. The series' four-color, accessible format makes the books attractive and inviting to readers of all levels. In addition, each viewpoint has been carefully edited to maximize a reader's understanding of the content. Short but thorough viewpoints capture the essence of an argument. A substantial, thought-provoking essay question placed at the end of each viewpoint asks the student to further investigate the issues raised in the viewpoint, compare and contrast two authors' arguments, or consider how one might go about forming an opinion on the topic at hand. Each viewpoint contains sidebars that include at-a-glance information and handy statistics. A Facts About section located in the back of the book further supplies students with relevant facts and figures.

Following in the tradition of the Opposing Viewpoints series, Greenhaven Press continues to provide readers with invaluable exposure to the controversial issues that shape our world. As John Stuart Mill once wrote: "The only way in which a human being can make some approach to knowing the whole of a subject is by hearing what can be said about it by persons of every variety of opinion and studying all modes in which it can be looked at by every character of mind. No wise man ever acquired his wisdom in any mode but this." It is to this principle that Introducing Issues with Opposing Viewpoints books are dedicated.

Introduction

"It's important that we begin the conversation about the society we want to create, and the role that drugs will play in that."

—David Nutt, chairman, Independent Scientific Committee on Drugs

In the autumn of 2012 sixteen-year-old Emily Bauer of Cypress, Texas, was with a group of her friends when they bought a package of a substance called "Kush" at a local gas station. Labeled as potpourri, this substance was unregulated and available for purchase by anyone. Emily had smoked marijuana before, and she expected Kush—a mix of dried herbs sprayed with chemicals (synthetic cannabinoids)—to result in a marijuana-like high that was legal.

Within fifteen minutes of smoking the substance, Emily told a friend that she had a migraine and needed to go home to take a nap. Over the next several weeks, as Emily continued to use synthetic marijuana, these headaches recurred. On December 7 she began hallucinating, stumbling, slurring her words, urinating on herself, and acting violently. By the following day—as she attempted to bite those trying to help her—paramedics had to restrain Emily during an ambulance ride to the hospital. Physicians put her into a coma to run tests on her brain. They discovered that Emily had suffered several strokes and had also developed vasculitis, an inflammation of blood vessels that limited the flow of blood and oxygen to her brain. Emergency surgery was performed to relieve the inflammation, but doctors saw that Emily had extensive, life-threatening brain damage. At one point, she was disconnected from life support. To her family's relief, she survived and regained consciousness. However, she remained blind, unable to feed herself, and unable to walk.

While most people who try synthetic marijuana will not experience the severe effects that Emily did, her story is a cautionary tale about the potential dangers of such "designer drugs." The makers of these drugs constantly change the mix of chemicals they use so that their product can bypass legal bans. Thus, those who buy these substances cannot really know what they contain, how potent they are, or how to avoid an overdose.

Synthetic drugs are not new. Technically, any artificially made chemical compound that affects the functioning of the body or mind is a synthetic drug. Today, however, the phrase "synthetic drugs" most often refers to human-made substances—usually (but not always) illegal—that are taken recreationally. Substances such as the hallucinogen LSD, the stimulant methamphetamine, and the club drug Ecstasy all fall into this category. Two groups of synthetic drugs that have come under scrutiny more recently include cannabinoid-mimicking compounds and mephedrones.

First synthesized in 1929, mephedrone is the human-made version of cathinone, the psychoactive ingredient in the African plant khat. In the early 2000s, mephedrone was used primarily as a pesticide in Israel. Scientists had observed that the chemical weakened certain insects, making them easier prey for predators—and causing no environmental damage. Mephedrone quickly became a popular party drug in Israel, however, when its psychoactive effects were discovered. Known by the nicknames "plant food" and "meow-meow," it was typically sold as a white powder marked "not for human consumption"—enabling it to bypass food safety laws. Israel banned mephedrone in 2007, but by 2009 it had become a sought-after club drug in the United Kingdom. The substance acts both as a stimulant and a mild psychedelic, producing feelings of euphoria, confidence, and exhilaration as well as a greater sense of openness to and empathy for others. It can also cause irregular heartbeat, dizziness, paranoia, insomnia, and—in extreme cases—panic attacks, seizures, and strokes. In 2010 all synthetic cathinones were banned in the United Kingdom. Following suit, the US Drug Enforcement Administration (DEA) issued an emergency ban on several chemicals used to make a similar synthetic cathinone known as bath salts in 2011.

While bath salts tend to be associated with raves and dance clubs, synthetic marijuana—also known as "spice"—has even broader appeal among a younger crowd. Among US middle school and high school students, for example, spice is (following natural marijuana) the second most frequently used illegal drug. In part, this is because its chemicals have been marketed as a "legal" alternative to marijuana, is sold in gas stations and mini-marts, and is packaged in eye-catching containers that tend to attract youth. Since spice is not detected in urine, those who are subject to drug tests see it as a way to get high without breaking the law and without jeopardizing their jobs.

Recreational synthetic cannabis first emerged in Europe in 2004, where it was produced and marketed under the brand name Spice by the Psyche Deli, a now-defunct company in London. Its popularity over the next several years encouraged competitors to create new cannabis-mimicking chemicals—all of which also went under the name spice. By 2012 more than fifty synthetic cannabinoids had been identified. These cannabinoids are mixed with a liquid, sprayed onto dried plant material, and labeled as "herbal incense" or "potpourri" by sellers. Smoking the substance creates effects similar to that of marijuana: elevated mood, relaxation, altered perceptions, and lowering of inhibitions. Many experts note, however, that spice products can be much more harmful than marijuana because their chemical mixtures and potencies vary widely. Some users have experienced chest pain, slurred speech, vomiting, panic attacks, heart problems, and psychotic episodes. Extreme adverse reactions, as in Bauer's case, include seizures and strokes.

Concerns about the safety of synthetic drugs have led to bans on these substances in several nations. In the United States, the Synthetic Drug Abuse Prevention Act of 2012 permanently outlawed twenty-six types of synthetic cathinones and cannabinoids. In addition, an older law—the Controlled Substance Analogue Enforcement Act of 1986—allows the DEA to impose an emergency ban on any new substance that is chemically similar to an illegal drug. Thus, in April 2013, the DEA was able to quickly put a temporary ban on three more synthetic cannabinoids. This strategy allows the government to take these substances off the market while they are studied to determine what their legal status should be.

Critics of the US government's policy on synthetic drugs argue that outlaw manufacturers can stay one step ahead of the law by constantly changing their formulas. When one product is banned, two or three others immediately replace it until authorities also discover and ban the replacements. One nation, however, is trying an alternative approach. In 2013 the New Zealand parliament passed the Psychoactive Substances Bill, which requires makers of designer drugs to conduct tests proving that their products are safe before they can be sold. "While other countries are still blindly banning drug after drug, [this] bill will put New Zealand ahead of the game," says Ross Bell, director of the New Zealand Drug Foundation. "It is a comprehensive, pragmatic and innovative approach to address a complex problem."[1]

Matters are still complicated, though, by the fact that people can purchase designer drugs online, ducking the law. Only time will tell which regulations, if any, provide the best safeguards against the risks of synthetic drugs. As the contributors to this volume attest, the increasing number of these drugs makes for a complex, ever-changing controversy. By examining the perspectives in this text readers are invited to engage with one of today's most pressing issues.

Notes
1. Quoted in Madison Park, "New Zealand: Prove Recreational Drug Is Safe, Then You Can Sell," CNN.com, July 11, 2013. www.cnn .com.

Chapter 1

Are Synthetic Drugs Dangerous?

Ecstacy, the street name for the pill form of MDMA, is a highly controversial synthetic drug.

Synthetic Drugs Are Dangerous

Joseph Lee, as told to Join Together

"[Synthetic] drugs can have a severe, detrimental impact right away."

In the following viewpoint Join Together, a collaboration between the Boston University School of Public Health and the Partnership at Drugfree.org (formerly the Partnership for a Drug-Free America), interviews Joseph Lee, a psychiatrist at Hazelden, a Minnesota-based addiction-treatment center. Lee maintains that synthetic drugs are especially dangerous and unpredictable because they contain unknown chemical mixtures created by amateurs. These substances can have serious health effects, including heart problems and long-term psychotic reactions, he argues. Moreover, it is not only addicts who experience problems with synthetic drugs; as Lee explains, just one youthful experiment with such drugs can have immediate negative effects, including death. He concludes that youths should be much better educated about the risks of synthetic substances—and undergo regular drug screenings as well.

AS YOU READ, CONSIDER THE FOLLOWING QUESTIONS:
  1. Which synthetic drug is most popular among youths, in Lee's opinion?
  2. As stated by the author, where do teens go to buy synthetic drugs?
  3. According to Lee, what behavior increases the chance of having a bad reaction to synthetic drugs?

Join Together: What trends are you seeing in adolescent abuse of synthetic drugs? Which designer drugs are becoming most widely used?

Dr. Lee: Most often, Hazelden doesn't see young people who are addicted primarily to synthetic drugs, but we do see a lot of experimentation. Of synthetic drugs, marijuana seems to be the most popular agent, with bath salts and hallucinogens used less frequently.

The majority of these young people who come in for residential care at Hazelden are admitted due to use of another substance, but many have tried synthetic drugs at some point. There are many cases, however, where synthetics became the primary drug of choice.

The Dangers of Synthetic Drugs

Why is the increasing use of synthetic drugs so worrisome?

These drugs are particularly dangerous because amateur laboratories manufacture them and no one knows enough about the chemicals used to make these substances. There are a lot of chemicals marketed as synthetic cannabis that actually have different components. No one would really think about smoking a bath salt or potpourri on its own. The contaminants in these chemicals alone should raise concern. Each time someone uses a synthetic chemical, they have no way of knowing what they are putting into their body.

Reports from emergency room admissions and overdoses indicate that many kids are experiencing very serious negative reactions to synthetic substances, including heart problems, psychosis and agitation, and in rare cases, death. Personally, I have seen many kids develop psychotic symptoms that do not improve for months. Also, synthetic drugs are often manufactured to escape detection from standard urine drug screens.

Easy Access

How are teens getting access to these drugs?

In the past, kids would buy these drugs from the same head shops where they get paraphernalia for marijuana and tobacco. Now, increasingly kids are going online to buy drugs to avoid getting caught.

FAST FACT

In 2012 the American Association of Poison Control Centers reported 2,656 calls related to incidents involving "bath salts," a synthetic drug.

It is tough to monitor the Internet for illegal drug sales because state and federal laws are not all-encompassing. If the state or federal government bans one substance, manufacturers can make a small change to the chemical so the new product is no longer illegal. This challenge mirrors the difficulty of regulating the sale of other drugs online.

Youths Who Try Synthetic Drugs

Which types of teens are most likely to experiment with synthetic drugs and why?

Anyone can experiment with synthetic drugs. However, there are at least three demographics that parents should be particularly aware of:

- Young people are intrigued by synthetic drugs because they are experimental by nature at this age. Many don't intend to get addicted, but decide to use drugs simply because their "friends are doing it, too." There was a case in Blaine, Minnesota where kids ordered an ingestible, synthetic hallucinogen called "2 C-E" online and as a result of using it, one 19-year-old died and 10 more young people were hospitalized. This group may not have been addicted to drugs, but were "just" experimenting.
- Young people who are already in trouble with the law and are being monitored use synthetic drugs because they are often undetectable by standard screenings.
- Young people who seek peer-approval, perhaps a little more than what would be considered normal, are attracted to the idea that they can know more about synthetic drugs than others. This group receives a certain sense of authority and credibility among

their network by being the person who is either well-connected or has an arcane knowledge of obscure drugs. They will often try chemicals that others might not try in order to demonstrate their mastery.

Overall, we are making a dangerous mistake by waiting for kids to show the signs of addiction before we educate children about synthetic substances. These drugs can have a severe, detrimental impact right away. Many kids have problems with synthetic drugs who are not necessarily addicted to anything else. Addiction is not a prerequisite for having a problem with synthetic substances.

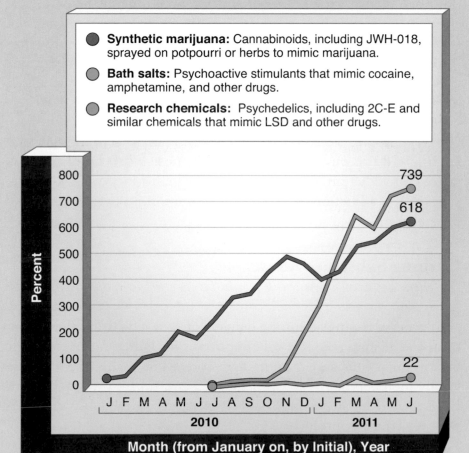

Calls to Poison Control Centers

Synthetic marijuana: Cannabinoids, including JWH-018, sprayed on potpourri or herbs to mimic marijuana.

Bath salts: Psychoactive stimulants that mimic cocaine, amphetamine, and other drugs.

Research chemicals: Psychedelics, including 2C-E and similar chemicals that mimic LSD and other drugs.

Taken from: American Association of Poison Control Centers. Drug Enforcement Administration, 2012.

Risky Behavior

Are these drugs being used alone or together with other drugs? Are they a "gateway" to other types of substance abuse?

It is normal, though not healthy, for kids to experiment with substances. That is one of the differences between young people and adults with drug abuse problems. However, this behavior is dangerous because they might find that one drug is more rewarding than another. It's just like ice cream: once they try and like chocolate ice cream, they wonder what strawberry ice cream tastes like. That's really their approach.

Often times, the fact that kids mix chemicals together with alcohol, cigarettes or other substances multiplies the risk of having a bad reaction. We see many examples of overdoses with alcohol and pain medication, but it can also occur with other substances. Kids are often falsely reassured by the amount of potentially bad information they get from online and other resources.

The so-called "gateway hypothesis" is controversial. Researchers cannot prove that the use of one drug does something in the brain that encourages the use of other drugs. However, we do know that when you track young people who use alcohol, marijuana, and other substances before the age of 15, they are more likely to experiment with and use other substances later on. We also know that the earlier a child abuses drugs, the more likely they are to develop an addiction later in life.

Many of the kids who use synthetic substances also seem to have behavior problems or other mental health issues at a young age, so it is important for physicians to screen for those kids who display risk factors for addiction. But, we also see very high-functioning kids who succumb to addiction due to experimentation, so every parent and physician must be cautious.

Curbing Substance Abuse

Are there any tactics you think would be effective in reducing the abuse of synthetic drugs?

Strong messaging about the dangers of synthetic drugs (and other drug and alcohol abuse) is very important for family members to use with their children at a young age. It is also equally essential that family members act in an open-minded and tolerant way with their children, so they feel comfortable coming to older family members with questions or problems.

It is true that parents who don't have strong messages about not using drugs often have kids who use more. Parents who are firm with expectations and limits, but who are also available emotionally have the most success. This is called authoritative parenting.

Parents also wait too long to screen their kids for drug use, and specifically synthetic drug use. They need to have regular screenings with their pediatrician and other health professionals, beginning at an early age.

Parents should take a close look at their family history. If they have a predisposition to substance abuse, they need to pay attention for their children. Additionally, if they have an older child who uses substances, that increases the risk that the younger child will use drugs, as well.

There are many other things that parents can do to help their child and plenty of comprehensive resources for them to access in their community and online.

EVALUATING THE AUTHOR'S ARGUMENTS:

In this viewpoint Joseph Lee discusses the "gateway hypothesis"—the notion that the use of one drug leads to the use of other drugs that may be more risky. Why is the gateway hypothesis controversial, according to Lee? Do you agree with his assertion that people are more likely to become drug addicts if they abuse drugs as children? Why or why not?

Mephedrone Ban Blamed for Rise in Cocaine Deaths

"Banning the 'dance drug' mephedrone may have cost lives rather than saving them—by driving users back to cocaine."

Jeremy Laurance

Jeremy Laurance is health editor for the *Independent,* a newspaper in the United Kingdom. In the following viewpoint Laurance reports on the recent publication of figures for drug-related deaths that show a decline in cocaine-related deaths during the period when the drug mephedrone was legal. One expert speculates that cocaine users switched to mephedrone when it was legal, resulting in a decrease in cocaine-related deaths. Another expert emphasizes that this opinion is just speculation.

AS YOU READ, CONSIDER THE FOLLOWING QUESTIONS:
1. As stated by the author, during what period of time did the deaths from cocaine and ecstasy decline?
2. According to the viewpoint, the recommendation from the Advisory Council on the Misuse of Drugs (ACMD) to ban mephedrone followed what event?
3. As stated in the article, how many cocaine fatalities occurred in the year prior to the decline in cocaine-related deaths? How many occurred during the year when cocaine-related deaths declined?

Banning the "dance drug" mephedrone may have cost lives rather than saving them—by driving users back to cocaine, an expert said yesterday.

Latest figures show deaths from cocaine and ecstasy fell during the first six months of 2009 at a time when the popularity of mephedrone, then still a "legal high", was rising. Separate evidence suggests that many drug users may have substituted it for cocaine, which could account for a decline in cocaine-related deaths.

Although mephedrone itself has been linked with several deaths, subsequent investigations have cast doubt on how dangerous it really is.

The ban on the drug was announced last March by former home secretary Alan Johnson after he received a recommendation from the Advisory Council on the Misuse of Drugs (ACMD). The decision followed a public outcry over the deaths of two teenagers—Louis Wainwright, 18, and Nicholas Smith, 19, from Scunthorpe—although toxicology tests later showed they had not taken the drug.

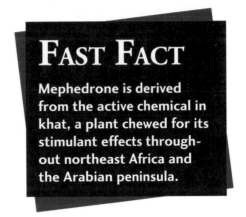

FAST FACT

Mephedrone is derived from the active chemical in khat, a plant chewed for its stimulant effects throughout northeast Africa and the Arabian peninsula.

Professor Sheila Bird, of the Medical Research Council's Biostatistics Unit in Cambridge, said yesterday that after rising for four years, deaths from cocaine fell in the first six months of 2009 to 66, a statistically significant drop from 95 in the same period of 2008. Delays in reporting drug-related deaths mean the figures have only now become available.

Writing on the website Straight Statistics, Professor Bird said mandatory drug tests carried out on soldiers by the army showed a sharp fall in cocaine use during 2008 which continued into 2009. "I speculated that this decline might be the result of soldiers' shifting to mephedrone, then a 'legal high'. If that were true among the wider drug-using population, then the decision in April 2010 to make mephedrone illegal may have had the unintended consequence of reversing a notable decrease in cocaine-related deaths," she wrote.

But Professor Leslie Iversen, chairman of the ACMD, dismissed the suggestion as "purely speculative". "There is also evidence that mephedrone was being used by young people who had never used drugs before. The poor quality of cocaine in the UK may have led people to mephedrone—but that is also speculation. There isn't any hard data," he said.

EVALUATING THE AUTHOR'S ARGUMENTS:

The viewpoint author, Jeremy Laurance, points to the co-occurrence of a decrease in cocaine-related deaths and the legal availability of another drug, as well as to one expert's speculation that the latter influenced the former, and to another expert's dismissal of the first expert's opinion as speculative and lacking data. Which expert do you agree with more? Why?

Viewpoint

3

Synthetic Marijuana Is Dangerous

Marc Lallanilla

"Synthetic marijuana ... is leaving a trail of dead and severely injured teenagers in its wake."

Synthetic marijuana is one of the most damaging drugs that has emerged in recent years, notes Marc Lallanilla in the following viewpoint. Also known as "K2" or "Spice," the United States banned the chemicals often used to make the drug in 2012 after numerous reports of its potential dangers, including violent behavior, brain damage, and death. However, as the author points out, makers of the drug have sidestepped the law by using different chemicals—thus no one really knows what substances synthetic marijuana may contain, or how potent it is. Despite its risks, the drug is increasingly popular, Lallanilla maintains. Lallanilla is an assistant editor for LiveScience, a science news website.

AS YOU READ, CONSIDER THE FOLLOWING QUESTIONS:
1. What happened to Emily Bauer after she smoked synthetic marijuana, as stated by Lallanilla?
2. In what form is synthetic marijuana often sold, according to the author?
3. According to Lallanilla, why do drug tests fail to detect synthetic marijuana?

Synthetic marijuana is cheap, readily available at convenience stores nationwide, and is leaving a trail of dead and severely injured teenagers in its wake, making it one of the most alarming new drugs available anywhere, according to medical experts and drug enforcement officials.

Dangerous Effects

Emily Bauer, a high-school sophomore from Cypress, Texas, reportedly had violent outbursts, urinated on herself, and showed psychotic behaviors, after smoking some synthetic marijuana last December [2012], according to CNN.com. Soon after, she was rushed to the emergency room at Northwest Cypress Hospital near Houston.

The following day, Emily was still behaving violently and injuring herself, according to the *Daily Mail*. Doctors decided to put the teenager in a medically induced coma to run tests on Emily's brain. That's when they discovered she had severe vasculitis—inflamed blood vessels in her head that had constricted, cutting off the supply of oxygen to her brain.

And when Emily's blood vessels started expanding again, they greatly increased the pressure on her brain, forcing surgeons to cut a hole in the teenagers skull and insert a tube to drain excess fluids and relieve the pressure.

FAST FACT

Synthetic marijuana is the second most widely used illegal drug among US tenth graders, according to the National Institute on Drug Abuse.

Subsequent brain images showed the extent of damage the girl had suffered. "We met with [the] neurology team who showed us Emily's brain images," her mother, Tonya Bauer, said on a Facebook page, according to CNN. "They told us that all white areas on [the] images were dead. It looked to us at least 70 percent of the images were white."

Much More Powerful than Marijuana

Synthetic marijuana is often sold as incense or potpourri, and can be branded with names like K2, Spice, Kush or Klimax, the *Daily Mail*

Synthetic marijuana is a mixture of various herbs, sprayed with an assortment of chemicals with effects that purportedly mimic the high from regular smoked marijuana.

reports. The substance is a mixture of various herbs, sprayed with an assortment of chemicals whose effects purportedly mimic the high from regular marijuana when smoked.

It was declared illegal in July 2012 after President Barack Obama signed legislation that banned five of the chemicals commonly used to make synthetic marijuana and bath salts, another dangerous drug concoction, CNN reports.

But manufacturers have evaded the ban by using different chemicals in their mixture, which adds to the dangers inherent in the drug: From one manufacturer to the next, and from week to week, doctors and drug-enforcement officials aren't sure what's in the stuff.

"It's really just an unknown. You don't know what you are going to get with every batch that you buy, and for that it can be extremely dangerous," an Oakland, Calif., undercover police officer told KTVU .com.

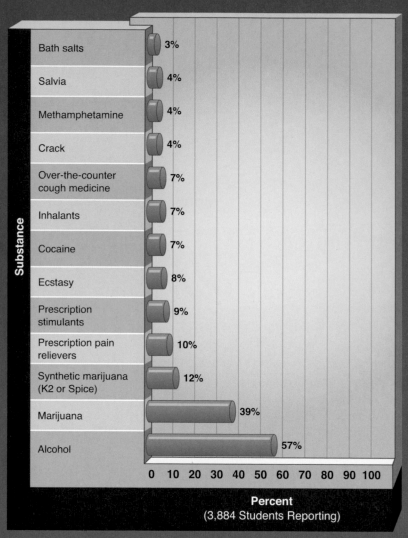

Percentage of US Students (Grades Nine to Twelve) Reporting Past-Year Alcohol and Other Drug Use, 2012

Substance	Percent
Bath salts	3%
Salvia	4%
Methamphetamine	4%
Crack	4%
Over-the-counter cough medicine	7%
Inhalants	7%
Cocaine	7%
Ecstasy	8%
Prescription stimulants	9%
Prescription pain relievers	10%
Synthetic marijuana (K2 or Spice)	12%
Marijuana	39%
Alcohol	57%

Percent
(3,884 Students Reporting)

Taken from: Adapted by CESAR from The Partnership for a Drug–Free America and the MetLife Foundation. *The Partnership Attitude Tracking Study (PATS): Teens and Parents,* 2013. Available online at http://www.drug free.org/newsroom/research-publication/full-report-and-key-findings-the-2012-partnership-attitude-tracking -study-sponsored-by-metlife-foundation.

An additional concern is that synthetic marijuana use can't be detected by urine tests, partly because the chemicals used in the drug change regularly.

"You're hearing some pretty bad things with the synthetic cannabinoids—part of that has to do with the potency," U.S. Drug

Enforcement Administration spokeswoman Barbara Carreno told CNN. "It can be 100 times more potent than marijuana."

And it's growing in popularity: One in every nine high school seniors admitted to having used synthetic marijuana in 2011, according to a University of Michigan survey—even though the substance was linked to more than 11,000 emergency-room [ER] visits in 2010. About one-third of those ER visits involved teens between ages 12 and 17.

"I Thought My Son Was Dying"

When Sidney Washington's mother came to pick him up from an after-school program in Oakland, Calif., earlier this year [2013], she found her 16-year-old son lying lifeless on the sidewalk, KTVU reports.

"I thought my son was dying. I thought that that was my last moment with him. I thought it was over," Latoya Washington told KTVU. Sidney recovered, but he's luckier than some users.

Emily, the Texas teenager, is now blind and partially paralyzed, though intensive therapy seems to be helping: She recently started moving her arms and legs again, and can once again eat solid food, the *Daily Mail* reports. But because of the extent of brain damage Emily suffered, doctors are unsure of how much Emily, now 17, can expect to recover.

Her parents have started a group called Synthetic Awareness For Emily (SAFE) to raise awareness of the dangers of synthetic marijuana.

"We want to let kids and parents know about the warnings signs," Emily's stepfather, Tommy Bryant, told the *Daily Mail.* "This synthetic weed stuff, it's so new that nobody knows about this stuff. We want to let other parents know about this so they don't have to go [through] what we've been going through."

EVALUATING THE AUTHOR'S ARGUMENTS:

Viewpoint author Marc Lallanilla opens with an anecdote about Emily Bauer, a Texas high school sophomore who suffered severe brain damage after smoking synthetic marijuana. Identify the other kinds of evidence he uses to support his argument that synthetic marijuana is dangerous. Do you find this evidence persuasive? Why or why not?

Authorities Should Avoid Overstating the Dangers of Synthetic Marijuana

Sharda Sekaran

"[Scare] tactics are ineffective at reducing teen drug use rates."

Sharda Sekaran is managing director of communications at the Drug Policy Alliance, an organization that advocates for drug policies grounded in science, health, and human rights. In the following viewpoint Sekaran decries the use of fabrications and scare tactics in ad campaigns intended to discourage teens from using synthetic marijuana. While youths should be warned about the potential risks of synthetic drugs, exaggerated claims do not reduce drug use or protect people from harm, Sekaran argues. Teens should instead be given science-based facts about drugs, she maintains.

AS YOU READ, CONSIDER THE FOLLOWING QUESTIONS:
1. Why is the film *Reefer Madness* a cult classic, according to the author?
2. What claims are made by the District of Columbia's advertising campaign against synthetic marijuana, according to Sekaran?
3. What should authorities do with synthetic marijuana, in the author's opinion?

You might be familiar with *Reefer Madness*, the drug war film from the 1930s that has become a cult classic because of its over-the-top scare tactics about marijuana. Generations have laughed at the film's cartoonish hysteria, with young students portrayed committing acts of violent lunacy after smoking a joint with their friends. Rather than educating young people about marijuana, *Reefer Madness* is widely seen as the epitome of unreliable and exaggerated propaganda.

The New *Reefer Madness*

The District of Columbia's Department of Health seems to have taken a page directly from *Reefer Madness* for its new advertising campaign, suggesting a synthetic form of marijuana known as "K2" or "Spice" will turn people who use it into "zombies." The ads recently made their debut on the

A current campaign that suggests a synthetic form of marijuana known as K2 or Spice will turn people who use it into "zombies" reminds the viewpoint author of the 1936 over-the-top antimarijuana movie Reefer Madness.

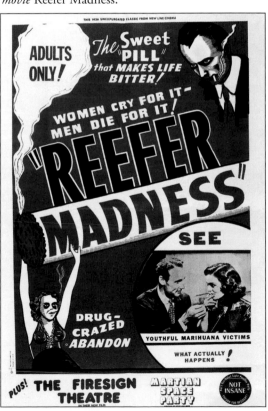

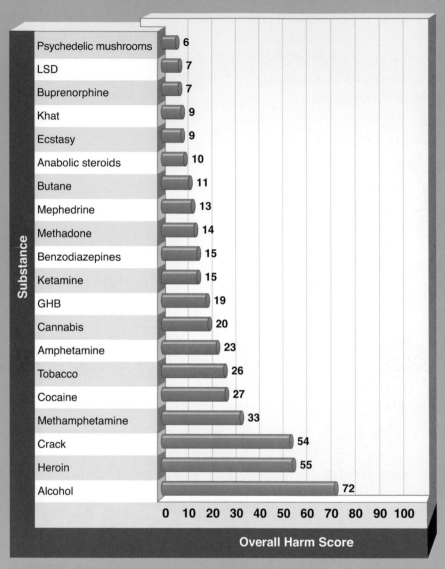

Relative Harms of Drugs

Substance	Overall Harm Score
Psychedelic mushrooms	6
LSD	7
Buprenorphine	7
Khat	9
Ecstasy	9
Anabolic steroids	10
Butane	11
Mephedrine	13
Methadone	14
Benzodiazepines	15
Ketamine	15
GHB	19
Cannabis	20
Amphetamine	23
Tobacco	26
Cocaine	27
Methamphetamine	33
Crack	54
Heroin	55
Alcohol	72

Taken from: David J. Nutt. et al. "Drug Harms in the UK: A Multicriteria Decision Analysis." *The Lancet*, 376, no. 9752, 2010, pp. 1558–1565.

DC Metro [trains and buses], and are wacky enough to look like a parody. Teenagers—presumably under the influence and grotesquely made up to look like "Walking Dead" [post-apocalyptic TV drama] extras—pose in various stages of decay with captions like "No One Wants to Take a Zombie to the Prom." Seriously?

Just about everyone agrees that teenagers should be discouraged from taking drugs and warned about potential health risks. But decades of exaggerated claims and egg frying commercials have taught us that wild and fictitious notions about drugs do very little to generate confidence, trust and safety among young people. Research by the Government Accountability Office, in fact, has found that these sorts of tactics are ineffective at reducing teen drug use rates.

A Sensible Alternative

There may be legitimate health concerns associated with synthetic marijuana, a chemical compound created to imitate the still-prohibited plant. Like any drug, "fake weed" should be carefully studied to better understand its effect on humans, and regulated accordingly. Giving teens access to information grounded in science and health is a much more sensible alternative to preparing them for the zombie apocalypse.

EVALUATING THE AUTHOR'S ARGUMENTS:

Viewpoint author Sharda Sekaran maintains that some authorities are making exaggerated claims about the dangers of synthetic marijuana in an attempt to dissuade youths from experimenting with the drug. Do you agree with her argument that these tactics do not reduce drug use? Why or why not?

Molly: Pure, but Not So Simple

Irina Aleksander

"'You're fooling yourself if you think [MDMA is] somehow safer because it's sold in powdered form.'"

In the following viewpoint Irina Aleksander explores the increasing popularity of powdered MDMA—a form of what was once called Ecstasy that has been nicknamed "Molly." Some patients in therapy received MDMA as a part of their treatment during the 1970s; by the 1980s and 1990s it had become a popular club drug known for inducing euphoria. In the early 2000s the drug fell out of favor as ecstasy pills became polluted with additives, the author explains. In recent years, however, powdered MDMA has emerged, boosted by claims that it is purer and safer than older versions of ecstasy. While the drug rarely causes death, it can have serious side effects, including hyperthermia, seizures, high blood pressure, and depression. In addition, some powders that are sold as Molly contain little or no MDMA, Aleksander notes. The substances may be dangerous synthetic mixtures that only mimic the effects of MDMA. Aleksander is a journalist whose work appears in the *New York Times*, *Atlantic Monthly*, and other periodicals.

AS YOU READ, CONSIDER THE FOLLOWING QUESTIONS:
1. What word is "Molly" derived from, according to the author?
2. According to Aleksander, what does the phrase "suicide Tuesdays" refer to?
3. In the opinion of Rick Doblin, as quoted by the author, why does MDMA appeal to people in today's electronic age?

A t a party not long ago in Park Slope, Brooklyn [New York], Kaitlin, a 22-year-old senior at Columbia University, was recalling the first time she was offered a drug called Molly, at the elegant Brooklyn home of a cultural figure she admired. "She was, like, 50, and she had been written about in the [prestigious *New Yorker* magazine column] Talk of the Town," said Kaitlin, who was wearing black skinny jeans and a tank top. "This woman was very smart and impressive."

At one point, the hostess pulled Kaitlin aside and asked if she had ever tried the drug, which is said to be pure MDMA, the ingredient typically combined with other substances in Ecstasy pills. "She said that it wasn't cut with anything and that I had nothing to worry about," said Kaitlin, who declined to give her last name because she is applying for jobs and does not want her association with the drug to scare off potential employers. "And then everyone at the party took it."

Since that first experience, Kaitlin has encountered Molly at a birthday celebration and at a dance party in Williamsburg. "It's the only drug I can think of that I have to pay for," she said. "It makes you really happy. It's very loose. You just get very turned on—not even sexually, but you just feel really upbeat and want to dance or whatever."

Not a New Drug

Molly is not new, exactly. MDMA, or 3,4-methylenedioxy-N-methylamphetamine, was patented by Merck pharmaceuticals in 1914 and did not make much news until the 1970s, when psychotherapists began giving it to patients to get them to open up. It arrived at New York nightclubs in the late 1980s, and by the early '90s it became the preferred drug at raves at Limelight and Shelter, where a weekly party called NASA later served as a backdrop in Larry Clark's movie "Kids."

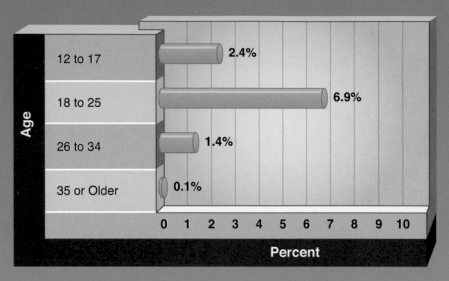

Percentage of People Reporting Ecstasy Use in 2001

Age	Percent
12 to 17	2.4%
18 to 25	6.9%
26 to 34	1.4%
35 or Older	0.1%

Taken from: National Household Survey on Drug Abuse, March 21, 2003.

Known for inducing feelings of euphoria, closeness and diminished anxiety, Ecstasy was quickly embraced by Wall Street traders and Chelsea [neighborhood] gallerinas. But as demand increased, so did the adulterants in each pill (caffeine, speed, ephedrine, ketamine, LSD, talcum powder and aspirin, to name a few), and by the new millennium, the drug's reputation had soured.

Then, sometime in the last decade, it returned to clubs as Molly, a powder or crystalline form of MDMA that implied greater purity and safety: Ecstasy re-branded as a gentler, more approachable drug. And thanks in part to that new friendly moniker, MDMA has found a new following in a generation of conscientious professionals who have never been to a rave and who are known for making careful choices in regard to their food, coffee and clothing. Much as marijuana enthusiasts of an earlier generation sang the virtues of Mary Jane [marijuana nickname], they argue that Molly (the name is thought to derive from "molecule") feels natural and basically harmless.

A 26-year-old New York woman named Elliot, who works in film, took Molly a few months ago at a friend's apartment and headed to dinner at Souen, the popular "macrobiotic, natural organic" restaurant in the East Village, and then went dancing. "I've always been somewhat terrified of drugs," she said. "But I'd been curious about Molly, which is sold as this pure, fun-loving drug. This is probably completely naïve, but I felt I wasn't putting as many scary chemicals into my body."

A Global Phenomenon

Robert Glatter, an emergency-room physician at Lenox Hill Hospital on the Upper East Side, might disagree. Dr. Glatter used to go months without hearing about Molly; now, he sees about four patients a month exhibiting its common side effects, which include teeth grinding, dehydration, anxiety, insomnia, fever and loss of appetite. (More dangerous ones include hyperthermia, uncontrollable seizures, high blood pressure and depression caused by a sudden drop in serotonin levels in the days after use, nicknamed Suicide Tuesdays.)

"Typically in the past we'd see rave kids, but now we're seeing more people into their 30s and 40s experimenting with it," Dr. Glatter said. "MDMA use has increased dramatically. It's really a global phenomenon now."

Nationally, the Drug Abuse Warning Network reports that the number of MDMA-related emergency-room visits have doubled since 2004. It is possible to overdose on MDMA, though when taken by itself, the drug rarely leads to death, Dr. Glatter said. (Official mortality figures are not available, but a study by New York City's deputy chief medical examiner determined that from 1997 to 2000, two people died solely because of MDMA.)

According to the United States Customs and Border Protection, there were 2,670 confiscations of MDMA in 2012, up from 186 in 2008.

"Oh, we're very aware of it," said Rusty Payne, an agent at the Drug Enforcement A[dministration]'s national office. Mr. Payne had not heard of Molly before 2008. Since then, the agency has used the term to document arrests in Syracuse [New York] and Jackson, Miss. "Molly has been very much glamorized in pop culture, which is obviously a problem," he said.

Promotion in Popular Culture

Indeed, many attribute MDMA's resurgence to the return of Electronic Dance Music (or E.D.M.), the pulsating Euro beat that has infiltrated the sound of pop radio acts like Rihanna, Ke$ha and Katy Perry. At the Ultra Music Festival in Miami last year [2012], Madonna was criticized for asking her audience, "How many people in this crowd have seen Molly?" (She later said that she was referring to a friend's song, not the drug.)

In the last year, rappers have also embraced Molly, with references to the drug appearing in lyrics by Gucci Mane, Kanye West and Lil Wayne, who raps, "Pop a Molly, smoke a blunt, that mean I'm a high roller," on Nicki Minaj's 2012 hit "Roman Reloaded." Rick Ross was recently dropped as a Reebok spokesman after he rapped about spiking a woman's champagne with Molly. And Miley Cyrus has a new single called "We Can't Stop," in which she sings what sounds like, "We like to party, dancing with Molly." (Her producer has said the lyric is "dancing with Miley.")

People who like Molly, which can cost $20 to $50 a dose, say it is a more socially acceptable drug than cocaine, because it is not physically addictive. Cat Marnell, 30, the former beauty director at xoJane.com who recently sold a memoir about drug addiction to Simon & Schuster for a reported $500,000, has noticed that many of her friends who sell Molly like to pack the powder into clear capsules that they buy from LifeThyme Market, the health food store next to C.O. Bigelow in the West Village. "Molly is the big thing now," Ms. Marnell said. "Coke is sort of grimy and passé. Weed smells too much and is also sort of low rent and junior high."

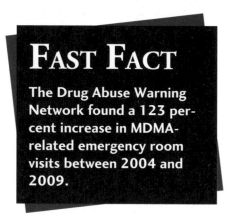

FAST FACT

The Drug Abuse Warning Network found a 123 percent increase in MDMA-related emergency room visits between 2004 and 2009.

But Ms. Marnell scoffed at MDMA's reformed image. "People think Molly is this flower-child drug," she said recalling photos from the 2011 Coachella music festival showing the former Disney star Vanessa Hudgens, wearing a floppy '70s hat and American Indian–inspired jewelry, dipping into a white powder that the gossip blogs ruled to be Molly. (Her publicist said it was white chocolate.) "It's true that it's not like cocaine in that it doesn't make you bloated and it doesn't make your nose raw, but sometimes you take it and you can't sleep or you get really sick. It's still a hard-core drug."

Madonna's references to "Molly" at the 2013 Ultra Music Festival drew criticism because some thought she was promoting the use of powdered MDMA, known as Molly.

A Greater Worry

MDMA was first classified as an illegal substance in 1985. By the early 2000s, public officials nicknamed Ecstasy "Agony," and warned that MDMA use could lead to Parkinson's disease, a lifetime of depression and "holes in your brain."

Those claims have since been disproved, according to Dr. John Halpern, a psychiatrist at Harvard who has conducted several MDMA studies. In recent years, the Food and Drug Administration has approved studies looking into whether MDMA can be used to treat post-traumatic stress disorder and anxiety in terminal cancer patients. And Dr. Halpern has found no evidence that the drug impairs cognitive performance. "A drug that actually does kill brain cells—which MDMA doesn't—is alcohol," he said.

But a greater worry for doctors and law enforcement officials is the many substances that people might be ingesting unknowingly when they take Molly. "Anyone can call something Molly to try to make sound less harmful," said Mr. Payne of the D.E.A. "But it can be anything."

According to Dr. Halpern, many of the powders sold as Molly contain no MDMA whatsoever; others are synthetic concoctions designed to mimic the drug's effects, Mr. Payne said. Despite promises of greater purity and potency, Molly, as its popularity had grown, is now thought to be as contaminated as Ecstasy once was.

"You're fooling yourself if you think it's somehow safer because it's sold in powdered form," Dr. Halpern said.

Why MDMA Is "Taking Hold"

But to some users, Molly still feels like a more respectable substance than others.

"I think people are much more aware of where coke comes from and what it does in those countries," said Sarah Nicole Prickett, 27, a writer for Vice and The New Inquiry, a culture and commentary site, who called cocaine a "blood drug." "Molly, if it's pure, it feels good and fun." (Much of it comes from Canada and the Netherlands, Mr. Payne said.)

Ms. Prickett, who moved to New York from Toronto last year, added that she could see why the drug might be taking hold in her new habitat.

"My impression of New York was that everyone just did drugs for work, that everyone was on speed," she said. "Molly makes you feel unplanned, and that's not a common feeling in New York, where everyone knows where they're going all the time and they're going very, very fast."

Rick Doblin, the founder of the Multidisciplinary Association for Psychedelic Studies, which has helped finance MDMA studies since the drug first entered the club scene, put Molly in the context of past drug trends: in the 1960s, he suggested, people searched for deeper spirituality and found LSD; in the '70s, as hippie culture became mainstream, marijuana entered the suburban household; in the '80s, cocaine complemented the extravagance and selfishness of the greed decade; and by the early '90s, youths dropped out of reality, dancing all night on Ecstasy or slumping in the corner on heroin. MDMA, which in addition to acting as a stimulant also promotes feelings of bonding and human connection, just might be what people are looking for right now.

"As we move more and more electronic, people are extremely hungry for the opposite: human interaction on a deeper level where you're not rushing around," Mr. Doblin said. "The rise of Molly is in tune with how people are feeling emotionally."

EVALUATING THE AUTHOR'S ARGUMENTS:

In this viewpoint author Irina Aleksander notes that MDMA has become glamorized in pop culture, particularly in electronic dance music and in rap songs. Some experts that she cites maintain that musical stars' references to "Molly" are to blame for the drug's increased popularity. Do you agree or disagree with this assertion? Explain.

MDMA Can Have Some Benefits

> "Because of MDMA's unique effect of diminishing fear and enhancing interpersonal trust, it is an ideal adjunct medicine to psycho-therapy."

Drug Policy Alliance

The following viewpoint is excerpted from an article by the Drug Policy Alliance, an advocacy organization that promotes science- and health-based drug policies. MDMA, traditionally known as Ecstasy, combines the effects of stimulants and hallucinogens, resulting in reduced anxiety, heightened sensations, feelings of connection to others, and euphoria. According to the author, MDMA overdoses are very rare; bad effects of the drug are usually linked to dehydration and high body temperature caused by physical exertion (usually dancing at clubs). MDMA's fear-reducing and empathy-enhancing properties make it beneficial for psychotherapy, the author contends. Trauma patients, for example, have found MDMA helpful in treating severe anxiety.

AS YOU READ, CONSIDER THE FOLLOWING QUESTIONS:
1. How long does a typical dose of MDMA last, according to the Drug Policy Alliance?
2. What is the RAVE Act, as stated by the author?
3. According to the author, what percentage of people over age twelve reported using MDMA during 2012–2013?

MDMA (3,4-methylenedioxymethamphetamine), commonly referred to as ecstasy, is sold either as a pressed pill taken orally, or as a powder that is snorted or swallowed. MDMA's effects resemble those of both stimulants and psychedelics. It is reported to decrease fear and increase trust and empathy. Street names include ecstasy; E; X; Rolls; Adam; Molly.

People who use ecstasy describe themselves as feeling open, accepting, unafraid and connected to people around them. Typically used in social settings, especially among the rave and dance club cultures, ecstasy's effects are stimulated by visuals, sounds, smells and touch. A typical dose of 100 to 125 mg lasts four to six hours. Some people experience nausea at the outset, but after about forty-five minutes, most people report feelings of relaxation and clarity. Ecstasy causes dilation of the pupils and, often, sensitivity to light. Jaw-clenching and tooth-grinding are also observable effects. People using ecstasy experience heightened sensations and want to intensify these feelings by dancing, talking and touching.

Before MDMA became popular at clubs and raves, it was utilized for therapeutic purposes by psychologists and other mental health practitioners in the 1970s and early 1980s. After MDMA was placed

Patient and therapist in psychotherapy. The viewpoint author believes MDMA is an ideal adjunct for psychotherapy because it reduces fear and enhances empathy.

in Schedule I [where the most addictive drugs not having any medical value are placed] in 1985, a lawsuit challenging this designation won a favorable ruling from the DEA [Drug Enforcement Administration] Administrative Law Judge, who concluded that MDMA had "currently accepted medical use" and "acceptable safety", yet it remains in Schedule I today. In 2002, the RAVE Act ("Reducing Americans' Vulnerability to Ecstasy") increased penalties and mandatory minimum sentences.

Prevalence of MDMA Use

According to the *National Survey on Drug Use and Health*, only 0.2 percent of people aged 12 and older reported using MDMA in the past year [2012–2013]. Among young people aged 12–17, 0.4 percent reported using it in the past month, and 1.7 percent in the past year.

Less than one percent (0.8) of students in 8th, 10th and 12th grades combined reported using ecstasy in the past month, according to the annual *Monitoring the Future* survey, while 35.9 percent of 12th graders reported that it is "fairly easy" or "very easy" to obtain.

> ## FAST FACT
>
> MDMA floods the brain with serotonin, a body chemical associated with feelings of alertness, happiness, and well-being.

Reducing Potential Harms of MDMA Misuse

Because ecstasy is illegal—and, therefore, unregulated—it is impossible to know what a "dose" contains. In fact, many ecstasy pills are not MDMA. Besides MDMA, ecstasy pills may contain varying levels of MDA (methylene-dioxyamphetamine), other stimulants such as caffeine, or anesthetics such as Ketamine or dextromethorphan (DXM)—which can significantly amplify potential harms. Testing kits are available to detect if pills contain MDMA or another substance, but cannot determine potency or purity.

Most of MDMA's potential harms derive from the setting of its use. Although few adverse effects have been reported, hyperthermia—a dangerously high increase in body temperature—is the most common problem related to ecstasy. Hyperthermic reactions result from physical exertion (such as dancing) in an overheated environment without replenishing

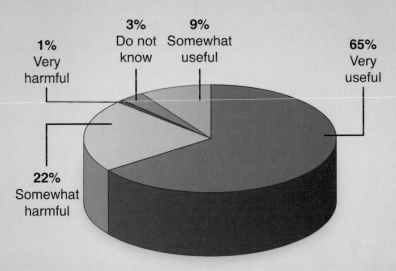

Has Ecstasy Been Useful in Your Life?

1%
Very
harmful

3%
Do not
know

9%
Somewhat
useful

65%
Very
useful

22%
Somewhat
harmful

Total Respondents: 923

Taken from: Erowid Ecstasy Safety Survey. www.erowid.org, 2002.

fluids, which is why users take breaks and consume fluids like water or Gatorade. Overdoses are extremely rare and are also usually linked to dehydration or mixing drugs, rather than as a direct result of using ecstasy.

Some people report feeling depressed for up to 48 hours after using. With prolonged use, people report tiredness, jaw aches and diminished euphoria.

Long-term effects of ecstasy are still under investigation. Some researchers suggest that slight brain changes may result from heavy use, but the evidence is far from conclusive. Ecstasy may affect serotonin and dopamine levels, but it is unclear what impact these changes cause in the long-term. Ecstasy can cause arrhythmia [irregular heartbeat] and those experiencing hypertension or heart disease should avoid using it. MDMA use alone does not cause cognitive differences between people who use it and those who do not. Evidence [garnered by researcher John E. Fisk and others] also shows that "[a]dverse effects decrease with . . . abstinence." Several studies have found that substances like MDMA have far lower potential to cause harm than legal drugs like alcohol.

Medical and Therapeutic Applications

MDMA-assisted psychotherapy combines traditional psychotherapy with the administration of MDMA. Because of MDMA's unique effect of diminishing fear and enhancing interpersonal trust, it is an ideal adjunct medicine to psychotherapy, and it has been administered to over 500 human subjects in clinical trials without a single serious adverse event. A seminal study published in 2010 found that PTSD [post-traumatic stress disorder] patients who received MDMA-assisted psychotherapy reported overwhelming reductions in the severity of their symptoms—reductions which were sustained, on average, for more than three years. Such findings have been replicated by other studies, and additional research is underway in the U.S., Canada, Israel, U.K. [United Kingdom] and Australia. Yet the drug war continues to obstruct this vital research.

EVALUATING THE AUTHOR'S ARGUMENTS:

The author of this viewpoint, the Drug Policy Alliance, is an advocacy organization that supports sensible drug policy reforms in the United States, with hopes of reducing the harms of both drug use and drug prohibition. How do the credentials of this author influence your appraisal of its viewpoint?

New Synthetic Drugs Are a Growing Global Threat

Fiona Harvey

"Massive expansion of the [synthetic drug] trade . . . has attracted the attention of international drug gangs."

International gangs are increasingly drawn to manufacturing and trafficking synthetic drugs, which is a growing threat worldwide, argues Fiona Harvey in the following viewpoint. In many nations, the use of "traditional" recreational drugs, such as marijuana, is on the decline, while the demand for prescription drugs and new psychoactive substances is on the rise. Furthermore, new synthetic drugs remain legal in some countries, where large factories can manufacture them in bulk and sell them around the world over the Internet, Harvey contends. Some law enforcement authorities are now calling for more international cooperation in identifying, tracking, and banning new psychoactive substances; they also support increased efforts to prevent and treat the abuse of synthetic drugs. Harvey is an environmental correspondent for *The Guardian*, a British daily newspaper.

AS YOU READ, CONSIDER THE FOLLOWING QUESTIONS:
1. According to Brian Nichols, as quoted by the author, why are drugs such as marijuana losing favor among international drug traffickers?
2. How many new psychoactive substances have been identified in recent years, as stated by the author?
3. In the United States, what does the scheduling of analogues accomplish, according to Harvey?

I nternational criminal gangs are rapidly expanding into the burgeoning market for new types of legal highs, while law enforcement agencies lack the tools needed to keep up, the head of US overseas drug enforcement has warned.

Governments have struggled to keep up with the rapidly growing market for new psychoactive substances, as banning a new drug can require a complex legislative process and many of these drugs remain legal in some countries, said Brian Nichols, assistant secretary at the US Bureau of International Narcotics and Law Enforcement Affairs.

FAST FACT

According to the UN Office on Drugs and Crime, in 2011 there were an estimated 211,000 drug-related deaths worldwide.

"These types of drugs are what transnational criminal networks are increasingly moving towards. Traditional drugs like marijuana are not as much in favour—they are bulky and hard to transport. Heroin and cocaine are very important but drug addiction is moving to the illicit use of pharmaceuticals and new substances like GBH," he told the *Guardian*.

"This is the growing threat. The use of traditional drugs is declining in the UK [United Kingdom] and the US, cocaine use is dropping, but prescription drug abuse is growing and new substance abuse is growing."

A Lucrative Market

Websites offering new psychoactive substances, marketed as bath salts or plant foods, are proliferating, thanks in part to the failure of law enforcement agencies to keep up with the range of new chemicals. Dealers remain a step ahead of the law by slightly altering the formula for known molecules such as MDMA (ecstasy), ketamine or LSD to create new drugs. They can be far more dangerous than traditional drugs, because they have not been widely tested on the street and because the difference between a dose that supplies a high and one that results in fatality can be extremely small.

What was once a cottage industry has rapidly evolved, with labs and factories in China, Europe and the US manufacturing the chemicals on an industrial basis, churning out hundreds of tonnes of the compounds

Michigan attorney general Jennifer Granholm holds a manufacturing kit for the date rape drug GHB. The drug is just one of a rapidly growing list of synthetic substances authorities are struggling to keep ahead of.

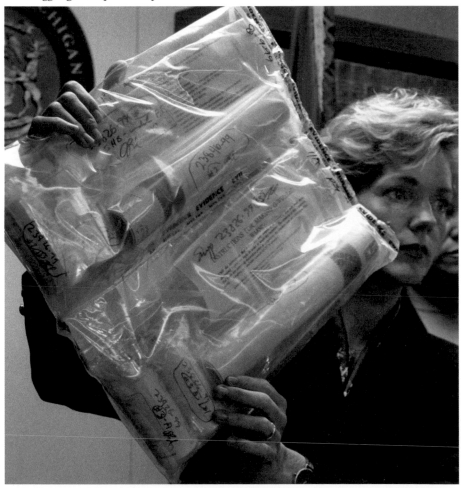

and selling them over the Internet. It is this massive expansion of the trade that has attracted the attention of international drug gangs, who use their expertise in trafficking traditional drugs such as heroin and cocaine to move into a new and lucrative market, said Nichols.

"There was a period of time in the US when you had new substances each week. Now you have by some counts well over 200 psychoactives [that] have been identified. It's my belief there are many more out there. We do not have people testing everything they come across," Nichols warned.

The Internet Factor

As with some other areas of international crime, such as wildlife trafficking, for which Nichols is also responsible, the rise of the Internet has been a central factor.

"Cybercrime means people can order up crime online. It is a greater globalisation [of crime] than we have ever seen before," said Nichols.

But many of the buyers do not realise how dangerous the substances they are taking can be. "Some of these party drugs are an incredible high at the right dosage, but if you take [a fractional amount more] then you have an incredible toxin," Nichols said.

The Need for International Cooperation

Nichols wants other countries to follow the lead of the US by bringing in legislation to fast-track the banning of new drugs. In the US, a process known as the scheduling of analogues allows drugs that are similar in effect or chemical make-up to existing illegal drugs to be banned without a lengthy process.

He also called for much more international co-operation in tracking and identifying new drugs and trying to prevent their distribution.

"One of the efforts we are pioneering in the UK and other partners in the G8 [the top eight economies around the globe] is encouraging the World Health Organisation to dedicate increased resources to identifying and scheduling of new psychoactive substances [and] create a more robust regime." He said there would also be an emphasis on demand reduction and treatment as well as preventing the sale and use of such drugs, and that help would be made available to countries lacking expertise in these areas.

Illicit Drug Use Is on the Decline

"Former 'legal highs' such as mephedrone and the cannabis substitute Spice . . . are no longer the fashionable drugs they once were."

Alan Travis

In countries such as England and Wales, illegal drug use is decreasing, asserts Alan Travis in the following viewpoint. Recent surveys reveal that drug use among sixteen- to twenty-four-year-olds has fallen significantly over the past decade. While synthetic drugs such as "bath salts" and synthetic marijuana were initially popular, researchers note that the use of these substances has also declined. Drug abuse remains a problem that needs to be addressed, but those who claim that the use of illegal substances is skyrocketing are exaggerating, the author concludes. Travis is the home affairs editor at *The Guardian*, a daily British newspaper.

AS YOU READ, CONSIDER THE FOLLOWING QUESTIONS:

1. As stated by Travis, what percent of the English population between age sixteen and fifty-nine took an illicit drug from 2010 to 2011?
2. What are the most popular drugs in England and Wales, according to the author?
3. According to the research group Drugscope, cited by the author, what factors are responsible for the general decline in illicit drug use?

I llicit drug use in England and Wales is firmly on a downward curve, with the latest annual figures confirming the long-term trend that they might simply be "going out of fashion".

The latest figures published on Thursday [September 27, 2012,] even record a decline in recently banned so-called "legal highs" such as mephedrone and Spice (synthetic cannabis).

The 2010/11 Home Office [the cabinet-level department of the British government overseeing affairs within Britain's borders] figures—which show that an estimated 3 million people, or about 9% of the population aged 16 to 59, have taken an illicit drug in the past year—have stabilised at the lowest level since the survey began in 1996.

The figures from the annual crime survey for England and Wales show that cannabis remains the most popular drug, with around 2.3

The author contends that the use of illicit synthetic drugs such as Spice has declined in recent years.

Use of Licit Versus Illicit Psychoactive Substances Among Youth and the Adult Population

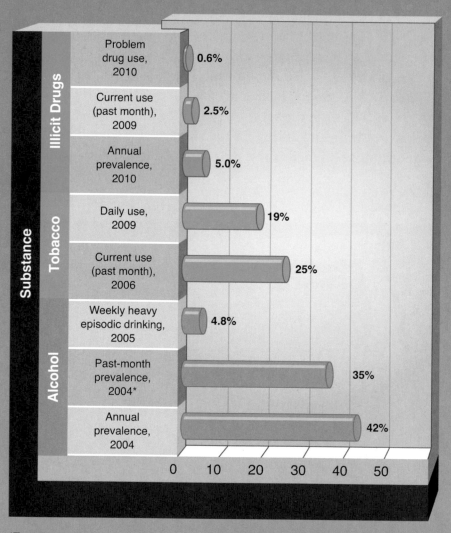

*Tentative estimate

Taken from: Estimates for illicit drugs based on UNODC data from the annual report questionnaire; alcohol statistics: World Health Organization, *Global Status Report on Alcohol and Health* (Geneva, 2011); and *Global Health Risks: Mortality and Burden of Disease Attributable to Selected Major Risks* (Geneva 2009); tobacco statistics: World Health Organization, *World Health Statistics 2010* (Geneva 2010).

million people using it in the past year, followed by powder cocaine at 700,000, ecstasy at 500,000 and amphetamines at 300,000.

They also show a continuing and stable low-level use of heroin at just 0.1% although use of the heroin substitute methadone has doubled over the past two years, from 0.1% to 0.2%.

Lower Rates of Drug Use Among Youths

The figures for younger people aged 16 to 24 show a similar pattern, with 19% saying they had used an illicit drug in the past year—again the lowest level since the survey began in 1996.

The long-term figures for this age group show that cannabis use has fallen sharply from 26% in 1996 to 15.7% last year, followed by a drop in powder cocaine use from 5.5% at its peak in 2009/10 to 4.2% last year. Despite the current media focus on ecstasy, its use among young people has also experienced a recent decline, down from 4.4% in 2008/09 to 3.3% in the latest figures.

Even former "legal highs" such as mephedrone and the cannabis substitute Spice, which enjoyed a brief period of popularity before being banned, are no longer the fashionable drugs they once were. Mephedrone remains as popular as ecstasy among young people, with 3.3% of 16- to- 24-year-olds using it in the past year, but even this is a decline since last year's survey showed 4.4% trying it.

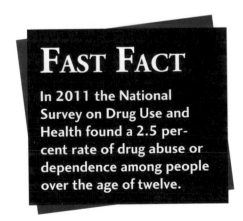

FAST FACT

In 2011 the National Survey on Drug Use and Health found a 2.5 percent rate of drug abuse or dependence among people over the age of twelve.

A Downward Curve

Harry Shapiro, editor of *Druglink* magazine, said that for the first time since drugs became a political issue in the 1960s most ways of measuring drug use were now on a firm downward curve.

In an editorial in this month's issue, published on Thursday [September 27, 2012,] by Drugscope, the leading independent centre of drugs experts, he says the substantial increase in drug treatment, the booming economy between 2000–08, and the relative strength of modern day cannabis may all be factors.

"More generally, drug use having become more normalised in society, might then be just as prey to fashion as any other cultural artefact. Drugs don't appear to be 'cool' these days as they once were," writes Shapiro.

He acknowledges that it is still a significant issue, with 300,000 serious problem drug users and rising youth unemployment, but "to suggest, as some do, that we are currently going to a drug hell in a handcart is just a wilful refusal to acknowledge the facts". Shapiro is particularly critical of politicians who repeatedly claim that drug use is spiralling out of control for their own purposes.

The Home Office figures published on Thursday also show that the most commonly reported age for first taking cannabis is 16, with people first trying cocaine and ecstasy at 18. Most have stopped using cannabis by the time they are 18 and stopped using cocaine or ecstasy by the time they are 25. A very small minority continue to use cannabis through their lives, with some reporting that they were still using cannabis at 59.

EVALUATING THE AUTHOR'S ARGUMENTS:

The author of this viewpoint, Alan Travis, contends that illegal drug use—including the use of newer synthetic drugs—is on the decline. This contradicts some assertions made in the previous viewpoint by Fiona Harvey. In your opinion, what might account for this contradiction? Do you find one of these two viewpoints to be more persuasive than the other? Or are you equally persuaded by both viewpoints? Explain.

Chapter 2

Should Synthetic Drugs Be Used Therapeutically?

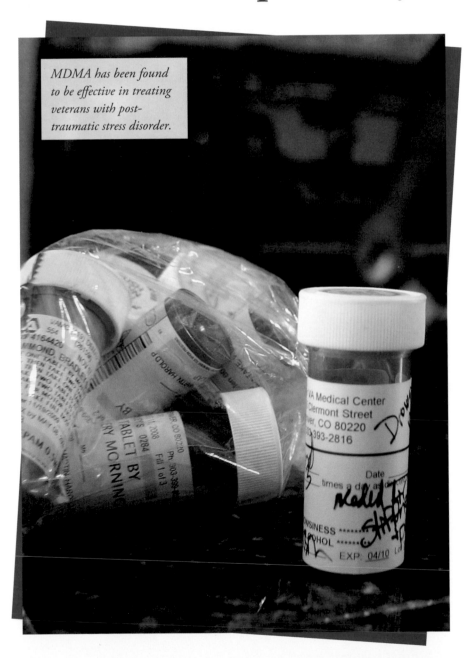

MDMA has been found to be effective in treating veterans with post-traumatic stress disorder.

Viewpoint

1

Ecstasy (MDMA) Is Effective in the Treatment of Post-Traumatic Stress Disorder

David P. Ball

"In controlled doses . . . [and] in a safe environment, [MDMA] can be safely used as an adjunct in therapy."

Research in the United States and Canada suggests that MDMA is highly effective in the treatment of post-traumatic stress disorder (PTSD), argues David P. Ball in the following viewpoint. In one US study, most of the PTSD patients who were treated with both psychotherapy and MDMA recovered and remain symptom-free after two years. Proponents claim that MDMA eases anxiety, enhances empathy, and opens people up emotionally so that they can face and heal their fears, contends Ball. For trauma patients, MDMA seems to foster the kind of therapeutic progress that goes beyond what counseling and conventional medicines can do. Ball is a multimedia journalist whose work appears in the *National Post*, *Toronto Star*, and other Canadian publications.

AS YOU READ, CONSIDER THE FOLLOWING QUESTIONS:
1. What percentage of PTSD patients treated with MDMA in a US research study completely recovered, according to Ball?
2. What was therapist Andrew Feldmár's answer when asked if he had ever tried MDMA, as reported by Ball?
3. On what date was MDMA first patented, according to the author?

Exactly a century after ecstasy was first patented, Health Canada has approved the drug's import for the first Canadian study using the illegal substance in trauma survivors' therapy.

The decision to allow two Vancouver therapists to import nine grams of MDMA from a laboratory in Switzerland—one of only two such permitted facilities worldwide—will kickstart the first experiment with the euphoria-and-empathy-producing drug in B.C. [British Columbia] on Jan. 1, [2013,] according to a Health Canada email obtained by the *National Post*, dated Nov. 23, [2012].

"I don't know if we'll have to wait until the MDMA is actually in our hands, but we've got a whole list of people who want to come to do it," Dr. Ingrid Pacey, one of the researchers, told the *Post*. "There's a part of me that still doesn't quite believe it. When the MDMA arrives from Switzerland . . . when it finally lands on Canadian soil, then I'll be certain."

The B.C. study follows U.S. research by Medical University of South Carolina psychiatry professor Michael Mithoefer and wife Ann Mithoefer, a nurse. In the *Journal of Psychopharmacology*, they reported that more than 83% of several PTSD [post-traumatic stress disorder] patients treated with MDMA and therapy had completely recovered, "without evidence of harm." A follow-up study published last month [November 2012] found that the patients still had virtually no symptoms two years later.

"What the MDMA does, because of the physiological effects, it means you are in a present, fearless state—able to look at those events without being re-traumatized, and healing in the present what was the trauma of the past," Dr. Pacey said.

MDMA's Benefit in Therapy

For her research partner, psychologist Andrew Feldmár, ecstasy-assisted therapy's benefits are obvious.

"It brings you into the present," Mr. Feldmár said, "You don't worry about the past or the future. It opens your heart; you don't feel any shame.

"Something horrible is done to you, and an alarm starts ringing. You just don't know how to turn it off. Even though the war is over, or no one is torturing you, or no one is hurting you, the alarm is still ringing. With the help of MDMA and good therapy, good connection and good company, the alarm can be stilled."

Provincial Health Officer Dr. Perry Kendall said the local MDMA study is "good news" for treating trauma. He drew controversy in June [2012] by suggesting that pure, unadulterated ecstasy may not be harmful, and that punitive drug policies were not effective.

"If it's a successful intervention, then I think it deserves broader application," he said in a telephone interview. "What the psychiatrists are saying is that in controlled doses, with a pharmaceutically known product in a safe environment, it can be safely used as an adjunct in therapy.

"PTSD is clearly an issue—and clearly an issue for returning veterans. . . . Anything that would add a useful addition to any therapeutic armamentarium—particularly one that maybe we lack effective interventions for—would be welcomed here."

Controversial Medicine

Mr. Feldmár acknowledges that the use of such drugs in therapy is controversial.

The tall, bearded therapist grins, shrugging when the *National Post* asks if he has tried MDMA.

"That remains a mystery," he said. "I can't say that for the record.

"I already have enough trouble going to the States. I'm just hoping to get a waiver so I can go to the MAPS [Multidisciplinary Association for Psychedelic Studies] international conference and talk about all this."

Vancouver's experiment will involve 12 patients with severe PTSD—such as terrifying nightmares, flashbacks, severe anxiety and

Percent of Subjects Qualifying for PTSD Diagnosis

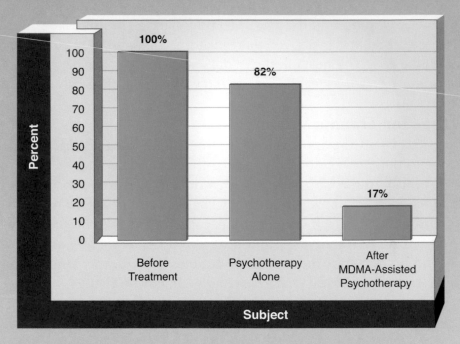

Taken from: Michael C. Mithoefer. "The Safety and Efficacy of ± 3, 4-methylenedioxymethamphetamine–Assisted Pyschotherapy in Subjects with Chronic, Treatment-Resistant Post-Traumatic Stress Disorder: The First Randomized Controlled Pilot Study." *Journal of Psychopharmacology*, April 2011.

a loss of trust. Each will take ecstasy in the counsellors' company, followed by eight hours of psychotherapy. After a supervised overnight stay, more therapy follows the next morning.

Ideally, Dr. Pacey said, the research staff will be able to try MDMA to understand its effects. Has she tried it herself?

"I took it before it was made illegal," she said. "I remember my first MDMA experience: it was magic; it was fabulous. It really did alter a lot of how I saw the world and myself. . . . It was beautiful—magical, even."

Authorization for Use of MDMA

MDMA was first patented on Dec. 24, 1912 by Merck pharmacologist Anton Köllisch. Canada banned the drug in 1976.

In November, it was upgraded from a Schedule III to a Schedule I substance, meaning that mandatory minimum sentences—and up to life in prison—would face those caught trafficking or producing it.

"Under the Controlled Drugs and Substances Act, authority is given to the minister of health to grant all authorizations to use a restricted drug for scientific research or other purposes," Health Canada spokesman Gary Holub told the *Post.* "To undertake a clinical trial using a restricted drug in Canada, certain regulatory requirements must be met.

"If the design of the clinical trial does not put the participants' safety at undue risk, then Health Canada allows the use of the study drug."

Hope for Trauma Victims

Dr. Pacey said the approval of the Vancouver research offers great hope to those psychologically scarred from trauma.

"A lot of my work has been with women—and some men—who had significant trauma, particularly sexual abuse, as children," she said.

"Initially, my work was mostly psychotherapy, with some use of traditional psychiatric medications. I found that I would work up to a certain point, but then make no progress. The deeper underlying fears and physiological changes are very difficult to change."

"My feeling is that the completion of therapy does require something that moves the person beyond their everyday reality. MDMA is a very effective way to really do that last piece of work, that traditional talk therapy and medication does not do."

Mr. Feldmár adds that there's no evidence that ecstasy is even addictive. "Some people consider it a sacrament," he said.

"You ask, 'Can you get addicted to it?' Do Catholics get addicted to the sacrament?

"One can get devoted, but that's not an addiction."

EVALUATING THE AUTHOR'S ARGUMENTS:

In this viewpoint David P. Ball cites researchers who contend that MDMA can be safely used in therapeutic environments to treat post-traumatic stress disorder. What evidence do these researchers offer in support of their argument? Are you convinced by this evidence? Explain.

Ecstasy (MDMA) Can Harm the Brain

Fiona Macrae

"Even low numbers of [ecstasy] pills [cause] memory problems."

Some recent studies conclude that MDMA is more damaging to the brain than previously thought, writes Fiona Macrae in the following article. According to researchers at the University of Cologne, Germany, even low amounts of the drug can cause memory lapses that resemble the early stages of dementia. These researchers are especially concerned that MDMA users may not recognize any sign of brain damage until it has already occurred. Macrae is a journalist who writes for the *Daily Mail*, a London newspaper.

AS YOU READ, CONSIDER THE FOLLOWING QUESTIONS:
1. According to the journal *Addiction*, cited by the author, how many MDMA pills a year are enough to cause damage?
2. What might have skewed the results of previous studies on MDMA use and memory, according to Macrae?
3. Since 1996, how many deaths have been linked to MDMA use in the United Kingdom, according to the author?

Taking ecstasy—even in relatively small amounts—can damage memory, scientists have warned.

Worryingly, the memory lapses are similar to those that occur in the early onset of dementia. Even ten pills a year—less than one a month—caused problems, says the journal *Addiction*.

Ecstasy, also known by its chemical name MDMA, is a Class A [termed "Schedule I" in the United States, the most dangerous class] drug. But there are disagreements over how dangerous it is. [United Kingdom] Government chief drugs advisor Professor David Nutt was fired three years ago [in 2009] after claiming taking ecstasy is no more dangerous than riding a horse.

MDMA Research

Although the drug's effects on memory have been studied before, results have been muddied by the possibility that users already had memory problems. To avoid this, researchers from the University of Cologne focused on young people who had tried the drug in the past and expected to use it more in future.

They were tested on their memory, learning, brain processing speed and attention at the start of the study and a year on. At the end of a year, 23 had become regular ecstasy users, having taken between ten and 62 ecstasy pills since the start of the study.

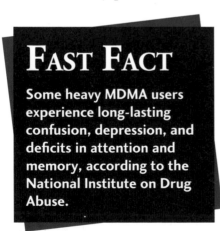

FAST FACT

Some heavy MDMA users experience long-lasting confusion, depression, and deficits in attention and memory, according to the National Institute on Drug Abuse.

Those who had become regular users showed a clear deterioration in episodic memory in comparison with the others. This memory details personal experiences, combining information about what happened with when and where—such as remembering not only the last film you saw but who you went with and where you sat. Lapses in it are seen as an indicator of the first stages of dementia.

Signs of Damage Show Up Later

Even low numbers of pills still caused memory problems. Importantly, users of ecstasy, which is also known as MDMA, may not realise their brain is being affected until the damage was done.

Effects of MDMA

Undesirable Effects	Potential Adverse Health Effects	Overdose Symptoms
Anxiety	Nausea	High blood pressure
Restlessness	Chills	Faintness
Irritability	Sweating	Panic attacks
Sadness	Involuntary jaw clenching and teeth grinding	Loss of consciousness
Impulsiveness	Muscle cramping	Seizures
Aggression	Blurred vision	
Sleep disturbances	Hyperthermia	
Lack of appetite	Dehydration	
Thirst	High blood pressure	
Reduced interest in sex	Heart failure	
Reduced mental abilities	Kidney failure	
	Arrhythmia	

A spokesman for the researchers said: 'As the nature of the impairments may not be immediately obvious to the user, it is possible people wouldn't get the signs that they are being damaged by the drug until it is too late.'

Lead author Dr Daniel Wagner, of the University of Cologne, said: 'By measuring the cognitive function of people with no history of ecstasy use and one year later identifying those who had used ecstasy

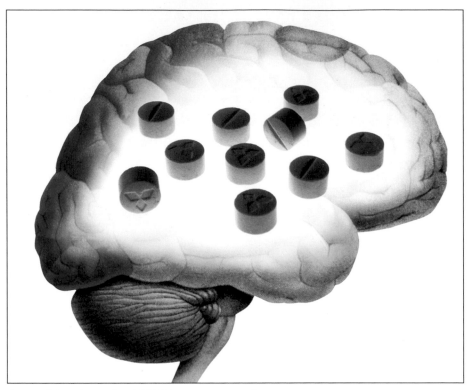

Research has shown that MDMA causes memory lapses.

at least ten times and re-measuring their performance, we have been able to start isolating the precise cognitive effects of this drug.'

'Our findings may raise concerns with regard to MDMA use, even in recreational amounts over a relatively short time period.'

Effects Are Usually Transient

Valerie Curran, professor of psychopharmacology at University College London, said that any effects on memory are likely to be small and transient. She said: 'The general agreement that is emerging about ecstasy is that while you are using the drug, you might expect a very subtle memory impairment but it's probably not significant in the real world'.

'When you stop using it, as most people do, things go back to the way they were.'

Young men and women in the UK are thought to be Europe's biggest users of ecstasy and the drug has been linked to more than 200 deaths since 1996.

Synthetic Medical Marijuana Is Safe and Effective

"The active ingredients in marijuana [can] be isolated and developed into a variety of pharmaceuticals, such as Marinol."

US Drug Enforcement Administration

In the following viewpoint the US Drug Enforcement Administration (DEA) argues the case for pharmaceutical use of synthetic marijuana, which has been approved by the Food and Drug Administration (FDA) for medical use. Marinol and Cesamet, available in pill form, contain synthetic forms of marijuana's active ingredients. These substances relieve the nausea and vomiting associated with chemotherapy and can also boost appetite in patients with AIDS. Smokable marijuana is not federally approved because the smoke contains hazardous chemicals and cancer-causing agents that can bring on additional health problems, the DEA maintains. The author also contends that it is difficult to deliver safe and effective doses of medicine in smoked form. The DEA enforces drug laws in the United States and coordinates US drug investigations in other countries.

"Marinol and Cesamet," US Drug Enforcement Administration, January 18 2012.

AS YOU READ, CONSIDER THE FOLLOWING QUESTIONS:
1. What is the name of the active ingredient in the medicine Cesamet, according to the author?
2. As stated by the DEA, how many chemicals are found in smoked marijuana?
3. When did the DEA first offer regulatory support for the study of marijuana's ingredients?

Pharmaceutical [marijuana] products already exist; they are called Marinol & Cesamet.

Marijuana's primary psychoactive ingredient delta-9-tetrahydrocannabinol (Delta9-THC) is controlled in schedule I of the Controlled Substances Act (CSA). According to Department of Human Health Services (DHHS), there are two drug products containing cannabinoid compounds that are structurally related to the active components in marijuana. Both are controlled under the CSA and both are pharmaceutical products, approved for marketing by the Food and Drug Administration (FDA).

Two Approved Synthetic Cannabinoids

1. A pharmaceutical product, Marinol, a schedule III drug, is widely available through prescription. It comes in the form of a pill and is also being studied by researchers for suitability via other delivery methods, such as an inhaler or patch. The active ingredient of Marinol is synthetic THC, which has been found to relieve the nausea and vomiting associated with chemotherapy for cancer patients and to assist with loss of appetite with AIDS patients.

2. Another FDA-approved medicine, Cesamet, a schedule II drug, is also available through prescription. It comes in the form of a capsule. The active ingredient of Cesamet is Nabilone, a synthetic cannabinoid, which has a chemical structure similar to THC, the active ingredient of marijuana. Cesamet was approved for marketing by the FDA in 1985 for the treatment of nausea and vomiting associated with cancer chemotherapy.

Marinol contains a legal synthetic form of THC, the active ingredient in marijuana. Marinol has been found to relieve the nausea and vomiting associated with chemotherapy and to counter the loss of appetite experienced by AIDS patients.

Unlike smoked marijuana—which contains more than 400 different chemicals, including most of the hazardous chemicals found in tobacco smoke—Marinol and Cesamet has been studied and approved by the medical community and the FDA, the nation's watchdog over unsafe and harmful food and drug products. Since the passage of the 1906 Pure Food and Drug Act, any drug that is marketed in the United States must undergo rigorous scientific testing. The approval process mandated by this act ensures that claims of safety and therapeutic value are supported by clinical evidence and keeps unsafe, ineffective, and dangerous drugs off the market.

Smoked Forms Are Unsafe

There are no FDA-approved medications that are smoked. For one thing, smoking is generally a poor way to deliver medicine. It is difficult to administer safe, regulated dosages of medicines in smoked form. Secondly, the harmful chemicals and carcinogens that are by-products of smoking create entirely new health problems. There are four times the level of tar in a marijuana cigarette, for example, than in a tobacco cigarette.

FAST FACT

Marinol takes effect about one hour after ingestion, and symptom relief lasts from four to six hours.

Or consider morphine, which has proven to be a medically valuable drug, but the FDA does not endorse the smoking of opium or heroin. Instead, scientists have extracted active ingredients from opium, which are sold as pharmaceutical products like morphine, codeine, hydrocodone or oxycodone. In a similar vein, the FDA has not approved smoking marijuana for medicinal purposes, but has approved the active ingredient—THC in the form of scientifically regulated Marinol.

The DEA helped facilitate the research on Marinol. The National Cancer Institute approached the DEA in the early 1980s regarding their study of THC in relieving nausea and vomiting. As a result, the DEA facilitated the registration and provided regulatory support and guidance for the study. California researchers are studying the potential use of marijuana and its ingredients on conditions such as multiple sclerosis and pain. At this time, however, neither the medical community nor the scientific community has found sufficient data to conclude that smoked marijuana is the best approach to dealing with these important medical issues.

The most comprehensive, scientifically rigorous review of studies of smoked marijuana was conducted by the Institute of Medicine, an organization chartered by the National Academy of Sciences. In

Misperceptions of Safety: Growing acceptance of medical marijuana may be influencing how young people perceive the harm associated with marijuana use generally. Research shows that as high school seniors' perception of marijuana's risks goes down, their marijuana use goes up, and vice versa.

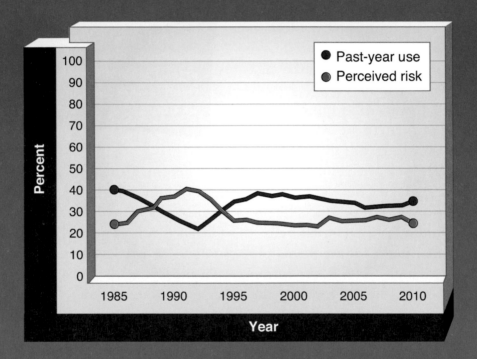

Taken from: "Drug Facts: Is Marijuana Medicine?" National Institute on Drug Abuse, July 2012. www.drugabuse.gov/publications/drugfacts/marijuana-medicine.

a report released in 1999, the Institute did not recommend the use of smoked marijuana, but did conclude that active ingredients in marijuana could be isolated and developed into a variety of pharmaceuticals, such as Marinol.

EVALUATING THE AUTHOR'S ARGUMENTS:

In this viewpoint the DEA uses an analogy to highlight a significant difference between Marinol (or Cesamet) and marijuana. Morphine, the agency points out, is a medically useful drug—but the smoking of opium or heroin remains illegal. Do you think this analogy convinces readers that Marinol is superior to smoked medical marijuana? Why or why not?

Synthetic Medical Marijuana Is Not as Effective as Smokable Marijuana

"Marinol ... is a less complex substance lacking ... some of the good components found in traditional marijuana."

Brian Montopoli

In the following viewpoint CBS News reporter and political analyst Brian Montopoli questions the claim that synthetic medical marijuana (Marinol) is superior to smokable medical marijuana. Proponents of Marinol argue that it does not contain the cancer-causing agents and other potential toxins found in marijuana smoke. However, as the author states, many patients who have tried both forms of medical marijuana find greater relief from nausea, vomiting, pain, and other symptoms from smokable cannabis. Marinol is ineffective in patients who are vomiting and cannot keep pills down; moreover, it is more difficult to control the dosage of Marinol. While smokable marijuana also has its drawbacks, the author maintains that it is dishonest to uphold Marinol as an effective alternative.

AS YOU READ, CONSIDER THE FOLLOWING QUESTIONS:
1. As stated by Montopoli, when did the Food and Drug Administration approve the prescribing of Marinol?
2. According to Mitch Earleywine, as quoted by the author, why does Marinol take longer to work than vaporized cannabis?
3. How much more does Marinol cost in comparison to smokable medical marijuana, according to Montopoli?

"Medical marijuana," the U.S. Drug Enforcement Administration says, "already exists."

They don't just mean in California. A pill known as Marinol has been legal and approved by the Food and Drug Administration for use with a prescription anywhere in America since 1985.

It's active ingredient? Dronabinol, better known as THC, the primary psychoactive element of the cannabis plant.

"Marinol provides standardized THC concentrations, does not contain the other 400 uncharacterized substances found in smoked marijuana, such as carcinogens or fungal spores, and is not associated with the quick high of smoked marijuana," said Neil Hirsch, a spokesman for Marinol manufacturer Solvay Pharmaceuticals.

Marinol Versus Smokable Marijuana

But Marinol is not the same thing as traditional, smokable marijuana. It is a less complex substance lacking both some of the good components found in traditional marijuana (such as cannabidiol, which has been found to have anti-seizure effects) and the bad or not-yet-fully-understood components (among them potential carcinogens) that can also come with the drug.

Ken Trainer, a 60-year-old Massachusetts resident who has battled Multiple Sclerosis for 25 years, said he has long been smoking marijuana to deal with the regular tremors he gets in his arms and legs.

"If I smoke a joint, the tremors go away most times before the joint is gone," he said. "It makes my life a little easier." Marinol, by contrast, "didn't really do much of anything for me," he said.

56-year-old Des Moines [Iowa] resident Jeff Elton, who was diagnosed with gastroparesis six years ago, had a similar experience when he was prescribed Marinol to deal with his chronic nausea and vomiting.

"I felt no relief, I didn't feel ill, I felt nothing," he said. "It might as well be M&M's [candies]."

Elton said he switched to marijuana, which he smokes through a vaporizer—a device that heats the active ingredients into a vapor instead of burning them. He said it allows him to keep down his food and regain some of the weight he lost while on Marinol.

The Pitfalls of Marinol

"[One] problem with Marinol is that it's orally administered," Dr. Mitch Earleywine, an associate professor of Clinical Psychology at the State University of New York at Albany, said in an email. "Therefore, it takes longer to work than cannabis inhaled from a vaporizer. (Usually 90 minutes at best rather than 15 seconds—a meaningful amount of time to the nauseated.)"

FAST FACT

Smoked medicinal marijuana takes effect five to fifteen minutes after ingestion and provides symptom relief for up to two hours, according to the Los Angeles Cannabis Resource Center.

"It's harder to control dosage, too, so folks end up discombobulated or without symptom relief," he added. "In addition, folks who are vomiting can't hold down the pills." Earleywine also said that a dose of Marinol costs three to five times as much as a comparable dose of medical marijuana.

Defenders note that Marinol is not meant to be a cure-all: It has been approved specifically for treating nausea and vomiting associated with cancer chemotherapy and for treating anorexia associated with weight loss in patients with AIDS.

"When the whole push for the smoked product came along, it was often for those two indications," said Dr. Herbert Kleber, a professor of Psychiatry at Columbia University and the former deputy drug czar

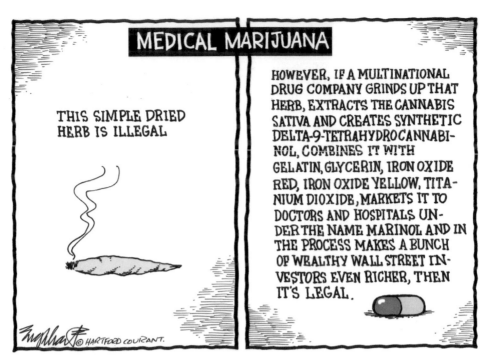

"Medical Marijuana," cartoon by Bob Englehart, *Hartford Courant*, PoliticalCartoons.com. Copyright © by Bob Englehart and PoliticalCartoons.com

under President George H.W. Bush. "And in general, I've not seen any need for the smoked form of marijuana for those two indications. Marinol had already been shown to be quite effective for those two things."

"Are there actions in the whole plant that you don't get from just the Marinol? I would be surprised if there wasn't," he continued. "The problem is that most of the data about the potential medical actions of the smoked form are anecdotal."

Ongoing Research

Research into the effects of medical marijuana is ongoing. The University of California, San Diego [UCSD], for example, boasts a Center for Medicinal Cannabis Research engaged in "focused controlled clinical trials on the efficacy of cannabis in patients diagnosed with HIV/AIDS, cancer, seizures or muscle spasms associated with a chronic debilitating condition, or any other serious condition providing sufficient theoretical justification." (The director of the UCSD program, Dr. Igor Grant, was out of the country and could not be reached for this story.)

The *Los Angeles Times*, which offers a nice overview of the current research, writes that "a growing body of research supports [medical marijuana's] medical usage, but some of it is cautionary." Marijuana has been found to be effective in counteracting severe pain, nausea and loss of appetite, though questions remain about the drawbacks, among them possible respiratory damage and increased cancer risk.

Dr. Kleber, who said he has prescribed Marinol to a patient and found it to be effective, points to what he characterizes as a significant advantage of the pill over traditional marijuana: "People don't abuse it."

"Marijuana addiction is becoming common and as a result I'm seeing an increasing number of people who have trouble stopping marijuana," he said. "Contrary to popular beliefs that there is no marijuana withdrawal, there is marijuana withdrawal. It's very clear cut."

The calculus, then, isn't quite as simple as the Drug Enforcement Administration suggests: Marinol and medical marijuana may share an active ingredient, but they offer somewhat different benefits and different drawbacks. Proponents of medicinal marijuana say it's disingenuous to hold up Marinol as a direct alternative to the more traditional form of the plant.

"I just don't understand how they won't let me smoke a joint, but they're more than happy to write me out prescriptions for anything that I want," Trainer said.

EVALUATING THE AUTHOR'S ARGUMENTS:

In this viewpoint Brian Montopoli compares the benefits of smokable medical marijuana against the benefits of Marinol, an approved synthetic pill form of marijuana. List the benefits and the drawbacks of both marijuana and Marinol. Do you think that the benefits of smokable marijuana outweigh its drawbacks? Why or why not? Cite the text in your answer.

Chapter 3

What Is the Best Way to Prevent Synthetic Drug Abuse?

These ketamine bottles confiscated by Chinese authorities are just the tip of the iceberg in the international drug trade of illicit synthetic drugs.

Synthetic Drugs Should Be Outlawed

Office of National Drug Control Policy

"51 new synthetic cannabinoids were identified in 2012, compared to just two in 2009."

The Office of National Drug Control Policy (ONDCP) advises the US president on drug-control issues, coordinates drug-control activities and related funding across the Federal government, and produces the annual National Drug Control Strategy, which outlines administration efforts to reduce illicit drug use, manufacturing and trafficking, drug-related crime and violence, and drug-related health consequences. In the following viewpoint the ONDCP discusses the history of synthetic drugs, the risk that they pose to the public health from a variety of chemicals not subject to regulatory oversight during manufacturing as well as from symptoms observed, and the steps that the government has taken to ban these synthetic substances.

AS YOU READ, CONSIDER THE FOLLOWING QUESTIONS:

1. As stated by the author, how are synthetic drugs labeled and for what purpose?
2. According to the viewpoint, what adverse health symptoms are associated with synthetic cannabinoids?
3. As stated in the article, the Synthetic Drug Abuse Prevention Act that is part of the FDA Safety and Innovation Act of 2012 placed how many types of synthetic cannabinoids and cathinones into Schedule I of the Controlled Substances Act (CSA)?

Office of National Drug Control Policy, "Synthetic Drugs (a.k.a. K2, Spice, Bath Salts, etc.)." www.white house.gov, 2013.

Synthetic cannabinoids, commonly known as "synthetic marijuana," "K2," or "Spice", are often sold in legal retail outlets as "herbal incense" or "potpourri", and synthetic cathinones are often sold as "bath salts" or "jewelry cleaner". They are labeled "not for human consumption" to mask their intended purpose and avoid Food and Drug Administration (FDA) regulatory oversight of the manufacturing process.

Synthetic cannabinoids are man-made chemicals that are applied (often sprayed) onto plant material and marketed as a "legal" high. Users claim that synthetic cannabinoids mimic Δ9-tetrahydrocannabinol (THC), the primary psychoactive active ingredient in marijuana.

Use of synthetic cannabinoids is alarmingly high, especially among young people. According to the 2012 Monitoring the Future survey of youth drug-use trends, one in nine 12th graders in America reported using synthetic cannabinoids in the past year. This rate, unchanged from 2011, puts synthetic cannabinoids as the second most frequently used illegal drug among high school seniors after marijuana.

Synthetic cathinones are man-made chemicals related to amphetamines. Synthetic cathinone products often consist of methylenedioxypyrovalerone (MDPV), mephedrone, and methylone.

The Administration has been working with Federal, Congressional, state, local, and non-governmental partners to put policies and legislation in place to combat this threat, and to educate people about the tremendous health risk posed by these substances.

A Rapidly Emerging Threat

Synthetic cannabinoids laced on plant material were first reported in the U.S. in December 2008, when a shipment of "Spice" was seized and analyzed by U.S. Customs and Border Protection (CBP) in Dayton, Ohio.

There is an increasingly expanding array of synthetic drugs available. 51 new synthetic cannabinoids were identified in 2012, compared to just two in 2009. Furthermore, 31 new synthetic cathinones were identified in 2012, compared to only four in 2009. In addition, 76 other synthetic compounds were identified in 2012, bringing the total number of new synthetic substances identified in 2012 to 158.

Risk to the Public Health

The contents and effects of synthetic cannabinoids and cathinones are unpredictable due to a constantly changing variety of chemicals used in manufacturing processes devoid of quality controls and government regulatory oversight.

Health warnings have been issued by numerous public health authorities and poison control centers describing the adverse health effects associated with the use of synthetic drugs.

The effects of synthetic cannabinoids include severe agitation and anxiety, nausea, vomiting, tachycardia (fast, racing heartbeat), elevated blood pressure, tremors and seizures, hallucinations, dilated pupils, and suicidal and other harmful thoughts and/or actions.

Similar to the adverse effects of cocaine, LSD, and methamphetamine, synthetic cathinone use is associated with increased heart rate and blood pressure, chest pain, extreme paranoia, hallucinations, delusions, and violent behavior, which causes users to harm themselves or others.

Sources and Continuing Availability

According to CBP, many synthetic cannabinoid and cathinone products originate overseas. Law enforcement personnel have also encountered the manufacture of synthetic drugs in the U.S., including in residential neighborhoods.

Synthetic drugs are often sold at small retail outlets and are readily available via the Internet. The chemical compositions of synthetic drugs are frequently altered in an attempt to avoid government bans.

Government Efforts to Ban Synthetic Drug Products

Congress has taken steps to ban many of these substances at the Federal level, and the Administration has supported such efforts.

The Synthetic Drug Abuse Prevention Act is part of the FDA Safety and Innovation Act of 2012, signed into law by President [Barack]

Obama. The law permanently places 26 types of synthetic cannabinoids and cathinones into Schedule I of the Controlled Substances Act (CSA). It also doubled the maximum period of time that the Drug Enforcement Administration (DEA) can administratively schedule substances under its emergency scheduling authority, from 18 to 36 months.

The Controlled Substance Analogue Enforcement Act of 1986 allows many synthetic drugs to be treated as controlled substances if they are proven to be chemically and/or pharmacologically similar to a Schedule I or Schedule II controlled substance.

In 2011, DEA exercised its emergency scheduling authority to control five types of synthetic cannabinoids, and three of the synthetic substances used to manufacture synthetic cathinones. In 2012, all but one of these substances were permanently designated as Schedule I substances under the Synthetic Drug Abuse Prevention Act, and the remaining substance was permanently placed into Schedule I by DEA regulation.

On April 12, 2013, DEA used its emergency scheduling authority to schedule three more types of synthetic cannabinoids, temporarily designating them as Schedule I substances.

At least 43 states have taken action to control one or more synthetic cannabinoids. Prior to 2010, synthetic cannabinoids were not controlled by any State or at the Federal level. In addition, at least 44 states have taken action to control one or more synthetic cathinones.

EVALUATING THE AUTHOR'S ARGUMENTS:

The author, Office of National Drug Control Policy, takes the position that synthetic drugs should be banned. What arguments do you think the author of the following viewpoint, an intern with an anti-drug-prohibition group, would present as a counter to this view? Which position do think is more persuasive? Why?

Outlawing Drugs Is Counter- productive

Christopher Soda

"These dangerous new substances exist only because of prohibition."

Prohibiting the use of recreational drugs is ineffective and dangerous, contends Christopher Soda in the following viewpoint. Despite decades of strict drug laws, the United States is still the world's largest consumer of illegal substances, the author notes. Furthermore, Soda argues, prohibition itself is to blame for the emergence of dangerous new synthetic drugs. When people are denied access to less-risky forms of intoxication, they turn to more dangerous substances that are readily available. Soda maintains that prohibitive US drug policies have created a kind of vicious cycle in which increasingly dangerous drugs emerge after lawmakers ban less-risky substances. Soda is an intern with the Drug Policy Alliance, an antiprohibition organization.

AS YOU READ, CONSIDER THE FOLLOWING QUESTIONS:
1. What are sumptuary laws, according to the author?
2. In the opinion of David Burns, as quoted by the author, how do people react when they feel pushed to do something?
3. What do drug prohibitionists fear will happen if banned drugs become legal, according to Soda?

I think it's safe to say most people were horrified upon hearing about [Texas teenager] Emily Bauer's close encounter with death after smoking synthetic cannabis. Some state governments, such as NJ [New Jersey] have recently adopted a ban on synthetic marijuana. Despite first impression, this is the approach to drug policy we need to distance ourselves from. Prohibition was sold on the pretense it could make society "safer." Let's be clear, these dangerous new substances exist only because of prohibition, the source of its many arms of harmful symptoms. Synthetic cannabis now gains a foothold in the dark corridors of the criminal underground.

According to a 2012 Report by The United States Senate Caucus on International Narcotics, *Reducing the Illicit U.S. Demand for Drugs*, "The United States continues to be the world's largest consumer of illegal drugs." Despite strict drug laws, demand is healthy as ever but why?

Prohibition Does Not Work
The system we've been applying for half a century is to coerce people to be moral by law. Many, like philosopher Alan Watts, liken these prohibitions under another instance of sumptuary law, which harken

The author asserts that drug prohibition has led to an increase in the emergence of dangerous new synthetic drugs, proving that the war on drugs has failed.

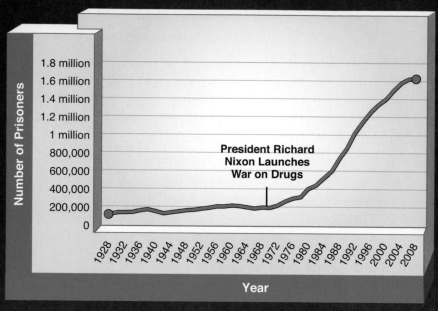

State and Federal Prison Population Before and After the Start of the War on Drugs, 1925–2010

President Richard
Nixon Launches
War on Drugs

Taken from: Bureau of Justice Statistics *Prisoner Series*.

back to Ancient Greece and Rome. Back then, sumptuary laws were often used to regulate dress to preserve a visual distinction between classes and assure people's consumption was befitting their station in life. Traditionally, they are any form of governmental control of consumption. Historically, these laws—like drug laws today—were largely ignored and almost impossible to enforce.

"Any time you feel shoved . . . you will attempt to exert your self-control and preserve your dignity by refusing to do the thing that you are being pushed to do," explains Dr. David Burns, critically-acclaimed author and adjunct professor in the Department of Psychiatry and Behavioral Sciences at the Stanford University School of Medicine. "The paradox is that you often end up hurting yourself."

When Will It End?

Apologists for prohibition contend that if we do reverse sumptuary laws drug use will explode, and society will fall apart. Dr. Kevin Sabet, a former senior adviser on drug policy at the White House, talks to this point when he says "marijuana legalization would expose us to unknown risk." But doesn't freedom involve risk? If the Pilgrims succumbed to fear and scary what-if scenarios, they never would have left the shores of Britain and colonized America. "Fear is good. Like self-doubt, fear is an indicator, says best-selling novelist Steven Pressfield. "Fear tells us what we have to do." It only becomes bad when we are unaware and give it control over our lives. The unknown is scary, but that's how progress is made.

FAST FACT

According to the Drug Policy Alliance, 1.53 million Americans were arrested on nonviolent drug charges in 2011.

Occurring at the same time voters in Colorado and Washington legalized marijuana, these synthetic cannabis bans are a reminder that prohibitionist policies still reign. These policies have fueled cartels, public health crises (HIV, overdoses), scores of needless death and disappearances, massive jail populations, and the emergence of new dangerous substances—like synthetic cannabis and bath salts. These symptoms are peripheral to the central driving source of prohibition and its incompatibility with basic human psychology. Despite prohibitive decrees, people will do drugs and the market will respond. "If you deny people access to the better ones, the ones they want," says Dr. Andrew Weil, "they'll turn to worse ones, ones that are more dangerous." To circumvent law, new dangerous substances will appear in the future and around we go again on the Prohibition Ferris-wheel. I find myself asking, "When will it end?"

EVALUATING THE AUTHOR'S ARGUMENTS:

In this viewpoint Christopher Soda argues that drug prohibition is impossible to enforce—and is dangerous as well. What evidence does he use to support this conclusion? Do you find his argument convincing? Explain.

Synthetic Drug Trafficking Organizations Should Be Targeted and Arrested

"Synthetic drug trafficking organizations . . . have operated without regard for the law or public safety."

US Drug Enforcement Administration

The US Drug Enforcement Administration (DEA), along with several law enforcement partners around the world, are seeking out and shutting down criminal organizations that traffic in synthetic drugs internationally. As the DEA contends in the following viewpoint, synthetic designer drugs are very dangerous, and the leaders of drug trafficking organizations have been profiting greatly while costing human lives. Through operations such as Project Synergy, the DEA and its partners have made hundreds of arrests, recovered millions of dollars, and seized large amounts of synthetic drugs. The DEA also supports emergency criminalization of any substance that mimics the effects of illegal drugs.

"Updated Results from DEA's Largest-Ever Global Synthetic Drug Takedown Yesterday," US Drug Enforcement Administration, June 26, 2013.

1. What other agencies coordinated with the DEA on Project Synergy, as stated by the DEA?
2. According to the Substance Abuse and Mental Health Services Administration, cited by the author, how many emergency room visits occurred because of synthetic marijuana in 2010? In 2011?
3. Under what names are synthetic cathinones sold, according to the DEA?

Yesterday [June 25, 2013,] the Drug Enforcement Administration (DEA) and its law enforcement partners announced enforcement operations in 35 states targeting the upper echelon of dangerous designer synthetic drug trafficking organizations that have operated without regard for the law or public safety.

These series of enforcement actions included retailers, wholesalers, and manufacturers. In addition, these investigations uncovered the massive flow of drug-related proceeds back to countries in the Middle East and elsewhere.

Project Synergy

Since Project Synergy began December 1 of 2012, more than 227 arrests were made and 416 search warrants served in 35 states, 49 cities and five countries, along with more than $51 million in cash and assets seized. Altogether, 9,445 kilograms of individually packaged, ready-to-sell synthetic drugs, 299 kilograms of cathinone drugs (the falsely labeled "bath salts"), 1,252 kilograms of cannabinoid drugs (used to make the so-called "fake pot" or herbal incense products), and 783 kilograms of treated plant material were seized.

Project Synergy was coordinated by DEA's Special Operations Division, working with the DEA Office of Diversion Control, and included cases led by DEA, U.S. Customs and Border Protection [CBP], U.S. Immigration and Customs Enforcement (ICE), Homeland Security Investigations (HSI), FBI, and IRS [Internal Revenue Service]. In addition, law enforcement in Australia, Barbados, Panama, and Canada participated, as well as countless state and local law enforcement members.

"Shutting down businesses that traffic in these drugs and attacking their operations worldwide is a priority for DEA and our law enforcement partners," said DEA Administrator Michele M. Leonhart. "These designer drugs are destructive, dangerous, and are destroying lives. DEA has been at the forefront of the battle against this trend and is targeting these new and emerging drugs with every scientific, legislative, and investigative tool at our disposal."

> ## FAST FACT
>
> In July 2013 New Zealand passed the Psychoactive Substances Bill, which requires all new recreational substances to pass governmental health regulations before they can be sold.

"CBP and DEA enjoy a close working relationship that was further enhanced through the collaboration of the National Targeting Center and CBP officers in the field at express consignment hubs during this operation to target, test and detain shipments of synthetic drugs, as well as precursor herbs used to manufacture synthetic marijuana," said CBP David Murphy, Acting Assistant Commissioner, Field Operations.

Scant Regard for Human Life

"The criminals behind the importation, distribution and selling of these drugs have scant regard for human life in their reckless pursuit of illicit profits," said Traci Lembke, HSI Deputy Assistant Director of Investigative Programs. "For criminal groups seeking to profit through the sale of illegal narcotics, the message is clear: we know how you operate; we know where you hide; and we will not stop until we bring you to justice."

"The harm inflicted by these designer drugs is matched only by the profit potential for those who sell them," said Richard Weber, Chief, IRS–Criminal Investigation [IRS-CI]. "Today's enforcement actions are the culmination of a multi-year effort in which IRS-CI worked with its domestic and global law enforcement partners to disrupt the flow of money—the lifeblood that allows these multi-million dollar organizations to proliferate."

"On behalf of the Australian Government, I congratulate the U.S. Drug Enforcement Administration and U.S. Customs and Border

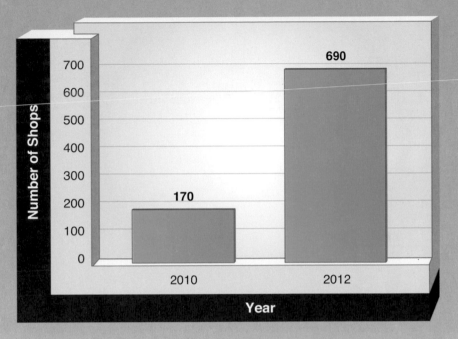

Online Shops Selling New Psychoactive Substances

Number of Shops

690

170

2010   2012

Year

Taken from: Organization of American States. "The Drug Problem in the Americas," 2013.

Protection on Project Synergy. This is a significant seizure of synthetic drugs and is a terrific result for our respective law enforcement agencies. Australia remains committed to sharing intelligence with its U.S. partners to combat transnational crime across international borders. This is a win for our collective communities," Australia's Acting Ambassador to the United States, Graham Fletcher, said.

Background on Designer Synthetic Drugs

Designer synthetic drugs are often marketed as herbal incense, bath salts, jewelry cleaner, or plant food, and have caused significant abuse, addiction, overdoses, and emergency room visits. Those who have abused synthetic drugs have suffered vomiting, anxiety, agitation, irritability, seizures, hallucinations, tachycardia [fast heartbeat], elevated blood pressure, and loss of consciousness. They have caused significant organ damage as well as overdose deaths.

A Drug Enforcement Administration spokesperson announces a nationwide synthetic drug bust in 2012, in which more than 227 arrests were made and 416 search warrants served in a thirty-five-city sweep.

Smokable herbal blends marketed as being "legal" and providing a marijuana-like high have become increasingly popular, particularly among teens and young adults, because they are easily available and, in many cases, they are more potent and dangerous than marijuana.

These products consist of plant material that has been impregnated with dangerous psychoactive compounds that mimic THC, the active ingredient in marijuana. Synthetic cannabinoids are sold at a variety of retail outlets, in head shops and over the Internet. Brands such as "Spice," "K2," "Blaze," and "Red X Dawn" are labeled as incense to mask their intended purpose. In 2012, a report by the Substance Abuse and Mental Health Services Administration (SAMHSA) reported 11,406 emergency department visits involving a synthetic cannabinoid product during 2010. In a 2013 report, SAMHSA reported the number of emergency department visits in 2011 involving a synthetic cannabinoid product had increased 2.5 times to 28,531. The American Association of Poison Control Centers reported 5,205 calls related to human exposure of synthetic cannabinoids.

For the past several years, there has also been a growing use of, and interest in, synthetic cathinones (stimulants/hallucinogens) sold under the guise of "bath salts" or "plant food." Marketed under names such as "Ivory Wave," "Purple Wave," "Vanilla Sky," or "Bliss," these products are comprised of a class of dangerous substances perceived to mimic cocaine, LSD, MDMA, and/or methamphetamine. Users have reported impaired perception, reduced motor control, disorientation, extreme paranoia, and violent episodes. The long-term physical and psychological effects of use are unknown but potentially severe. The American Association of Poison Control Centers reported 2,656 calls related to synthetic cathinone ("bath salts") exposures in 2012 and overdose deaths have been reported as well.

These products have become increasingly popular, particularly among teens and young adults and those who mistakenly believe they can bypass the drug testing protocols of employers and government agencies to protect public safety. They are sold at a variety of retail outlets, in head shops, and over the Internet. However, they have not been approved by the Food and Drug Administration (FDA) for human consumption or for medical use, and there is no oversight of the manufacturing process.

Controlled Substance Analogue Enforcement Act

While many of the designer drugs being marketed today that were seized as part of Project Synergy are not specifically prohibited in the Controlled Substances Act (CSA), the Controlled Substance Analogue Enforcement Act of 1986 (AEA) allows many of these drugs to be treated as controlled substances if they are proven to be chemically and/or pharmacologically similar to a Schedule I or Schedule II controlled substance. A number of cases that are part of Project Synergy will be prosecuted federally under this analogue provision, which is being utilized to combat these new and emerging designer drugs.

DEA has used its emergency scheduling authority to combat both synthetic cathinones (the so-called "bath salts" with names like Ivory Wave, etc.) and synthetic cannabinoids (the so-called incense products like K2, Spice, etc.), temporarily placing several of these dangerous chemicals into Schedule I of the CSA. Congress has also acted, permanently placing 26 substances into Schedule I of the CSA in 2012.

EVALUATING THE AUTHOR'S ARGUMENTS:

At the end of this viewpoint the DEA explains the purpose of the Controlled Substance Analogue Enforcement Act (AEA), which allows synthetic designer drugs to be treated as controlled substances if they share similarities to illegal drugs. How does this law enhance DEA-promoted operations such as Project Synergy? Do you think enforcement of the AEA can reduce the abuse of synthetic drugs, or do you think other strategies are called for? Explain your answer.

Synthetic Drug Use Should Be Restricted to Adults

Max Pemberton

"Perhaps it will be safer in the long term to restrict the use of these substances to adults."

Max Pemberton is the pen name of a British physician, journalist, and author. He works as a psychiatrist for the National Health Service and writes a column for the *Daily Telegraph*. Pemberton was curious about the effects of the synthetic drug mephedrone, which was still legal when he wrote this viewpoint. Along with two friends, he decided to take the drug as an experiment, and he enjoyed its euphoria-inducing effects. Pemberton still feels that taking mephedrone entails risks and that too little is known about its long-term effects. However, he also contends that it is futile to simply tell youths that synthetic drugs are dangerous. Many of them have tried these drugs and suffered no ill effects. Ultimately, he concludes, the best way to protect young people from potentially risky substances is to be honest with them about drugs and limit the use of intoxicants to adults.

AS YOU READ, CONSIDER THE FOLLOWING QUESTIONS:
1. Why did the author decide to try mephedrone?
2. What did Pemberton find most worrisome about mephedrone after his experience with it?
3. Why would Pemberton prefer that youths drink alcohol rather than take mephedrone?

L ast Saturday [in March 2010], I took drugs. This kind of behaviour does not constitute my usual type of weekend activity, I assure you. I am, after all, a doctor. As I stood with a rolled-up bank note in my hand, staring down at the thin line of white powder I was about to snort, I thought back to the innocent shopping trip earlier in the day that had led to this.

I'd been in central London buying a birthday card when I noticed a row of small packets on the counter by the till. They caught my eye and as I waited to pay I absent-mindedly picked one of them up. It was a folded piece of card, no bigger than the size of a book of stamps. The front was decorated in bright green and orange and it had pictures of flowers and the words "Buzz Gro". In tiny letters below it said: "water-soluble all-purpose plant food". On the inside was stapled a small transparent packet with a white powder inside.

"Plant Food"?

For a brief moment I was genuinely puzzled as to why a card shop was selling plant food. Then I suddenly realised, this wasn't plant food in the conventional, Baby Bio, sense. This was mephedrone, a "legal high" that has become increasingly popular as a cheap and easy alternative to illegal street drugs such as ecstasy or cocaine.

While it is marketed as "plant food", it is no such thing and this term is used only to avoid the Medicines Act, which makes it illegal to sell or advertise it for human consumption. It has been in the news this week after the tragic death of two teenagers in north Lincolnshire [England] who had taken it but, for the time being at least, it remains legal and, as I discovered, startlingly easy to procure.

I had first heard about the drug last summer [2009]. To start with, it was patients who incidentally reported taking it when I saw them in A&E [accident and emergency, a hospital emergency room] and asked about their drug use. They all raved about it and kept assuring me it was OK because it was legal. Then I began to hear whispers from friends. Respectable, sensible people told me they had tried it. And here, standing in a shop just a few hundred yards from Oxford Street on a crisp, spring afternoon, I'd stumbled across it for myself.

Out of curiosity I asked the cashier how much it was and he told me it was £19.99 [about US$40] a packet. I hesitated. "What do you do with it?" I asked. He rolled his eyes at me: "Snort it, put it in a drink or wrap it in paper and swallow it," he said with disinterest and put the earphones of his iPod back in.

"What are the side effects?" I asked. He didn't even remove his earphones and simply shrugged while he continued to chew his gum. No mention that nobody knows the long-term effects, the correct dose to take, what to expect from it or the risks. I've had better counselling buying Night Nurse [flu medicine].

An Experiment

Surely it can't be that bad if I can buy it in a shop, I reasoned to myself. But, more than anything, I felt I had to know what it was that so many of my patients were telling me they were taking each weekend. Impulsively I bought some. I was nervous, so before taking it, I canvassed a few friends. A lawyer, an architect and two people in publishing: they had all tried it and said how good it was. Back at home, my friends—a doctor and a midwife—arrived and after some discussion, we decided to try it.

At first, I felt nothing except a slight burning sensation in my nose. Then, as I went to the kitchen to get a drink, it occurred to me how much I loved my friend Rhiannon. I came back in and sat down on the chair and stared at her. "You OK?" she asked. "I am absolutely fine," I replied, smiling widely. "I really love you." "It's working then," she replied sardonically. A few minutes later, we were all sitting round in a euphoric haze, smiling benignly but with an incomprehensible, overwhelming desire to dance. It was nearly impossible to keep still.

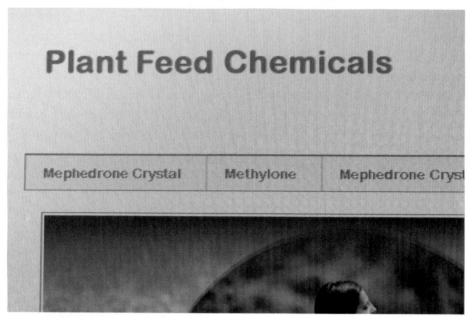

Mephedrone, a synthetic drug similar to the herb khat that is chewed by native Africans for its stimulant effect, has become popular in Great Britain.

Then things became very vivid and real and everything everyone said suddenly became very important. Before we knew it we were piling into a cab, laughing and giggling uncontrollably and going to a club. The effects lasted for about another two hours. Then, as suddenly as they had appeared, they vanished.

I was left standing in the club with a pounding headache, wondering what on earth had possessed me to go out. I can now understand why people re-dose as soon as the effects wear off because the contrast between being intoxicated and not is sharp and sudden.

Reasons for Concern

My prohibition on taking drugs until this point had been because they were illegal. I think that people should be free to make choices about their lives and that, providing they are aware of the consequences, this includes doing things that might damage their health. I am not a complete puritan—I smoke and drink. But my problem with illegal drugs is the human suffering that surrounds this market. Gun crime, prostitution, murder, extortion, burglary. It ruins lives and communities, and that's not something I want to buy into.

But mephedrone was different. There was a veneer of respectability about buying this drug and it was this, along with the complete ease with which I obtained it, that worried me afterwards. I didn't need a dealer or contacts. I hadn't even stumbled across it in the dark, sinister reaches of cyberspace. I'd wandered into a shop and picked it up as though it were a pair of novelty socks. This drug isn't even like alcohol or cigarettes, which have age restrictions on their use. Literally anyone can get hold of it and yet it is so new that we know next to nothing about its long-term effects.

Making this drug illegal will stop many of the people I know using it. It will also remove the implicit suggestion that because it's legal it must be safe. But I also know that simply making something illegal will not stop it being used, or indeed eradicate the need that people have to take substances that temporarily alter their experience of the world and intoxicate them.

Saying "Drugs Are Bad" Does Not Work

I do not take drug use lightly. I have worked in a clinic for people addicted to drugs and have often come across people who use drugs in my work in mental health. I have seen firsthand the devastating impact that substances have on people's lives.

I'd love to be able to tell you that I had a hideous time when I took mephedrone but the truth is, I didn't. It was a lovely feeling and I can completely understand why people would use it. Personally, I don't like the idea that I am having a good night because I've taken some-thing to make me feel as though I am enjoying myself; I like having a good night out because I actually am enjoying myself.

But this is a moot point for many youngsters, and it's them that I am particularly worried about because their concept of risk is so embryonic. It's futile telling teenagers that drugs are bad and are going to kill them. This doesn't work for the simple reason that they look at their peers who have taken it and survived, and come to the conclusion that adults are wrong and are trying to stop them from having a good time. This is further compounded if they do then dabble in drugs and find that, contrary to what they were told, they are actually very enjoyable.

Restricted Use Is Best

I do not doubt that mephedrone will be made illegal, and this is prob-ably a very sensible course of action if we want people to be as risk averse as possible. But what must be appreciated is that as soon as it is, it's only a matter of time before another substance appears, creating the same problems all over again.

There may come a point in the future where we tire of this cat-and-mouse game and accept that there is a need for a legally sanctioned stimulant. Perhaps it will be safer in the long term to restrict the use of these substances to adults, and license their sale and enable information to be gathered about their side effects, long-term health implications, dosing and risk minimisation.

All we can do at the moment is keep talking in an open and honest way to young people about drug use. I never thought I'd sanction this, but at present, I'd rather they drank alcohol, with all its known problems, than took plant food, with all its unknowns.

EVALUATING THE AUTHOR'S ARGUMENTS:

Viewpoint author Max Pemberton took mephedrone to see what it was like, and he admits that he largely enjoyed the experience. But he also writes that young people should avoid this and similar synthetic drugs. In your opinion, does his pleasant experience with mephedrone undercut his implied warning to youths about its potential risks? Why or why not?

A Vaccine Should Be Developed to Treat Methamphetamine Addiction

"If the vaccine proves effective in humans . . . it could become the first specific treatment for meth addiction."

Scripps Research Institute

In the following viewpoint the Scripps Research Institute shares some promising research on experimental vaccines for methamphetamine addiction. Six potential meth vaccines, developed by chemist Kim Janda, have been tested on rodents. One of them, referred to as MH6, works by blocking two common effects of a meth high: increased physical activity and a rise in body temperature. Another research group is focusing on meth "antibodies," which would, when injected in one concentrated dose, prevent a meth high for weeks at a time. As methamphetamine is one of the most addictive and commonly abused synthetic drugs, researchers hope to develop a cost-effective vaccine that lasts for months. Based in La Jolla, California, the Scripps Research Institute is a nonprofit organization that focuses on the biomedical sciences.

"News Release: Meth Vaccine Shows Promising Results in Early Tests," Scripps Research Institute, November 1, 2012. Copyright © 2012 by Scripps Research Institute. All rights reserved. Reproduced by permission.

AS YOU READ, CONSIDER THE FOLLOWING QUESTIONS:
1. How many people are affected by methamphetamine addiction worldwide, according to the author?
2. How many methamphetamine users are there in the United States, as stated by the Scripps Research Institute?
3. What is one drawback of the antibody-based therapy for meth addiction, in the author's opinion?

Scientists at The Scripps Research Institute (TSRI) have performed successful tests of an experimental methamphetamine vaccine on rats. Vaccinated animals that received the drug were largely protected from typical signs of meth intoxication. If the vaccine proves effective in humans too, it could become the first specific treatment for meth addiction, which is estimated to affect 25 million people worldwide.

"This is an early-stage study, but its results are comparable to those for other drug vaccines that have then gone to clinical trials," said Michael A. Taffe, an associate professor in TSRI's addiction science group, known as the Committee on the Neurobiology of Addictive Disorders. Taffe is the senior author of the study, which is currently in press with the journal *Biological Psychiatry*.

A Common and Dangerous Drug of Abuse

Over the past two decades, methamphetamine has become one of the most common drugs of abuse around the world. In the United States alone there are said to be more than 400,000 current users, and in some states, including California, meth accounts for more primary drug abuse treatment admissions than any other drug. Meth has characteristics that make it more addictive than other common drugs of abuse, and partly for this reason, there are no approved treatments for meth addiction.

In recent years, scientists at TSRI and other institutions have taken the innovative approach of developing vaccines against addictive drugs. These vaccines evoke antibody responses against drug molecules, just as traditional vaccines evoke antibody responses against viruses or bacteria. Anti-drug antibodies are meant to grab hold of drug molecules and keep them from getting into the brain—preventing the drug from giving the user a high and removing the incentive for taking the drug.

Vaccines against nicotine and cocaine are already in clinical trials. Some meth vaccines have been tested in animals, but generally with unpromising results. The methamphetamine molecule is structurally simple, making it relatively unnoticeable to the immune system. Meth and its main metabolite, ordinary amphetamine, also tend to linger once they get into the nervous system, so that even a little drug goes a long way. "The simple structure and long half-life of this drug make it a particularly difficult vaccine target," said Kim Janda, the Ely R. Callaway, Jr. Professor of Chemistry and member of the Skaggs Institute for Chemical Biology at TSRI.

"Encouraging Results"

Two years ago [in 2010] Janda and his laboratory developed six candidate meth vaccines. In each, the main active ingredient was a chemical cognate [similarly structured] of the methamphetamine molecule—that otherwise would be too small to evoke any antibody response—linked to a larger, antibody-provoking carrier molecule.

The effects of methamphetamine addiction can be readily seen in these pictures of one woman taken before her addiction and again after four years of being a meth addict.

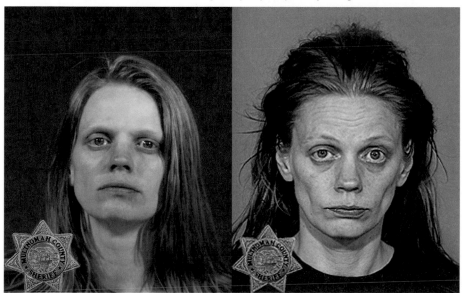

Early tests in mice indicated that three of these vaccine candidates could evoke a strong antibody response to meth. Taffe's laboratory later tested these three vaccines in rats and found the one, designated MH6, that worked best at blocking two typical effects of meth—an increase in physical activity and a loss of the usual ability to regulate body temperature.

In the new study, members of Taffe's laboratory, including Research Associate Michelle L. Miller, who was lead author of the study, investigated the MH6 vaccine in more depth. Using a different experimental setup, they found again that it prevented a rise in body temperature and burst of wheel-running hyperactivity that otherwise occur after meth exposure. Underlying these promising effects on behavioral measures was a robust antibody response, which in vaccinated rats kept more of the drug in the bloodstream and out of the nervous system, compared to control rats. "These are encouraging results that we'd like to follow up with further animal tests, and, we hope, with clinical tests in humans some day," said Miller.

FAST FACT

The annual retail value of the US methamphetamine market is an estimated $5 billion, according to the Organization of American States, an international alliance of nations in the Americas.

"I think that this vaccine has all the right features to allow it to move forward in development," said Janda. "It certainly works better than the other active vaccines for meth that have been reported so far."

The Next Big Challenge

A separate group of researchers has reported promising animal test results for an antibody-based treatment. In this approach, the anti-meth antibodies are grown in cultured cells using standard biotechnology methods and then injected into the animal in a concentrated dose, preventing a meth high. Antibody-based therapies are commonly used to treat cancer and chronic immunological conditions. But they are typically expensive, costing thousands of dollars per dose, and the effects of a dose last for a few weeks at most. A meth

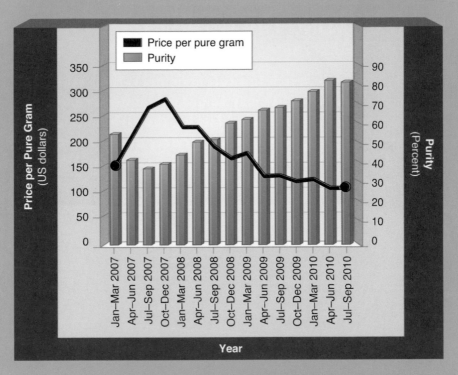

Mean Price and Purity of Methamphetamine Purchases by Law Enforcement Agencies in the United States, 2007–2010

Taken from: US, Department of Justice. *National Drug Intelligence Center, National Drug Threat Assessment 2011* (August 2011); US, Drug Enforcement Administration, System to Retrieve Information from Drug Evidence (STRIDE) database.

treatment probably would have to be much more cost-effective to be widely useful, as addicts frequently have little money and no health insurance and receive their treatments from government health services.

In principle, an active vaccine would be cheap to make and administer and would confer protection for months per dose, rather than weeks with conventional monoclonal antibody therapy. In practice, active meth vaccine candidates don't yet last that long; for example, the MH6 candidate in the current study was given in four doses over 12 weeks. But Janda and Taffe believe that with further adjustment, an active meth vaccine could sustain an anti-meth antibody response for a much longer period.

"Extending the duration of protection is the next big scientific challenge in this field," said Taffe.

EVALUATING THE AUTHOR'S ARGUMENTS:

The Scripps Research Institute examines various experimental vaccines that may someday counteract methampetamine addiction by blocking the high that users experience. Do you think that vaccines should be made widely available for use in treating drug addiction? Why or why not?

Viewpoint

6

Legalizing Natural Marijuana Would Curb the Abuse of Synthetic Marijuana

"People will continue to smoke unknown chemicals . . . endangering their lives and others in turn, all because what they really want to smoke is illegal."

Diane Kearns-Carlstrom

Synthetic marijuana is endangering lives, all because what users really want to smoke—marijuana—is illegal, contends Diane Kearns-Carlstrom in the following viewpoint. Commonly known as "spice," the drug mimics a marijuana high and will not show up in drug tests. Unlike marijuana, however, spice is addictive and can cause anxiety, hallucinations, violent aggression, seizures, and overdoses, the author argues. Spice was developed to skirt marijuana laws, but it is a much stronger and more dangerous drug than marijuana, which actually has medicinal properties, the author maintains. The author questions the continued illegality of marijuana, which she believes provides a safer high than spice does. Kearns-Carlstrom is a writer and journalist who advocates for the legalization of medical cannabis.

AS YOU READ, CONSIDER THE FOLLOWING QUESTIONS:
1. Where is today's synthetic marijuana usually made, according to the author?
2. What are the potentially dangerous side effects of spice, as stated by the author?
3. Why do many adults smoke synthetic marijuana, in Kearns-Carlstrom's opinion?

Today, teenagers and adults in our community are smoking a substance they consider to be synthetic marijuana. Typically called Spice, this stuff is a blend of herbs and chemicals that was created to mimic a marijuana high but will not show up during a urine analysis.

Last July [2011], Spice was made illegal in Florida, or maybe I should say the chemical compounds sprayed on it were made illegal. Florida Gov. Rick Scott also signed into law on March 23, 2012, a measure expanding the ban to make additional compounds illegal and already there is a new blend available that is in 'full compliance with the law'.

While its history is murky, we do know that Spice was being used in Europe during the 1990s, again as a way to skirt anti-marijuana laws. The Spice on today's market is usually made in Asia and sold in small local markets. Organic chemist John W. Huffman of Clemson University was studying cannabinoid receptors in the brain and wrote about his studies and [pharmaceutical giant] Pfizer created synthetic compounds designed to mimic cannabis.

From there, some adventurous soul figured out a way to make "fake marijuana." Spice is considerably stronger though, and as I will explain is very little like the herb it is trying to mimic.

Marijuana (cannabis) has a psychoactive ingredient called THC. This is what makes people feel high when they ingest it, but it also has many other ingredients that have helpful properties: anti-inflammatory, anti-emetic [prevents vomiting], anti-tumor, neuroprotective properties and much more. More than 3,000 studies in the last decade point to the many medical uses this plant has and a PubMed [biomedical literature] search on medical marijuana yields almost 2,500 hits.

Searching for "cannabis" and other like terms shows more.

Not Blowing Smoke

In 2003, the U.S. Government took a patent on some of these ingredients because it recognized the medical potential. Also, several drug companies are working on medicines to help several conditions, including MS [multiple sclerosis], chronic pain, psychiatric and others. The same cannot be said of Spice.

Cannabis is known mostly for its sedative effect (which varies) coupled with "munchies," which is a craving for certain food, lots of it, while Spice can cause aggression, extreme paranoia, anxiety, hallucinations, seizures and a host of other unpleasant effects. Those are just some side effects from using Spice.

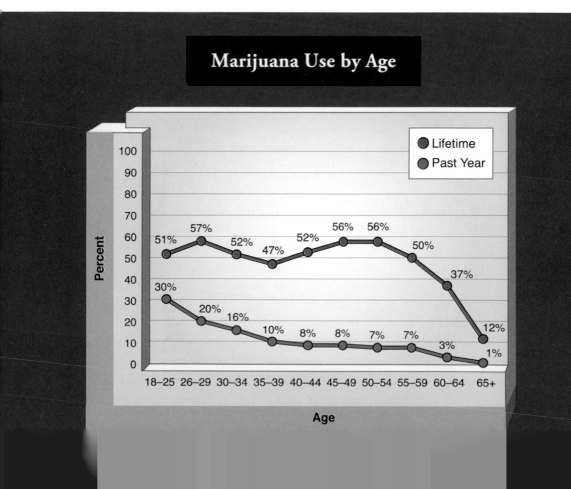

The most agitated a cannabis user would get while high is some disappointment the Twinkie box is empty, but that can be remedied with a Devil Dog or a slice of pizza. Not long after a nap will be in order. . . .

The Dangers of Spice

Police have had violent encounters with users [of Spice], and there have been plenty showing up in the emergency room with seizures, racing hearts and hallucinations. Some users become addicted to it. There has even been some deaths attributed to its use.

The first death in the Tampa Bay [Florida] area linked to Spice was that of Logan Kushner, a Pinellas County teenager, according to the *Tampa Bay Times*. That same story says that despite the new law, enforcing the ban on Spice chemicals is "tough." After a raid on a suspected synthetic marijuana manufacturer in Tampa April 4 [2012], deputies were waiting to see if samples matched up with the new list of banned chemicals.

Authorities have reportedly said they fear manufacturers could change chemicals used to make synthetic marijuana.

Surely people MUST know this stuff is dangerous! Not true.

People Are Told That All Drugs Are Bad

Many users are just kids who have constantly been told year after year, how bad drugs are. They are told to "Just Say No" and "Rise above peer pressure."

Well, kids have learned not all bad drugs are created equal. They aren't told the real facts behind abuse, why some people get carried away and others have no issue.

The lack of self-esteem that fuels abuse is not mentioned. Or cultural influences. Or countless other things.

They're just told all drugs are bad and will do terrible things to you, unless prescribed by a doctor.

A person holds cigarettes made from synthetic marijuana. Many feel synthetic marijuana is more dangerous than real marijuana because its ingredients continually vary.

It's not just the kids either. There are plenty of adults lighting up Spice. Spice won't show up if they get tested for work or for any other reason. Plenty have become ex-pot smokers and just smoke Spice now. I have yet to meet one who prefers it, but they reason they won't lose their job over something they did last Saturday night.

No One Has Ever Died from a Marijuana Overdose

I have written about some of the medical benefits of cannabis and will write more in days to come. Those aside, it has been established that cannabis does not do the harm that many drugs do.

According to former U.S. Surgeon General Jocelyn Elders in a Dec. 14, 2002, editorial published in the [Toronto, Canada] *Globe and Mail:*

> Tobacco, through its direct physical effects, kills many thousands of people every year. So does alcohol. And it is easy to fatally overdose on alcohol, just as you can fatally overdose on prescription drugs, or even over-the-counter drugs, such as aspirin or acetaminophen (the active ingredient in Tylenol). . . .

> I don't believe that anyone has ever died from a marijuana overdose.

A very recent study showed that smoking cannabis does not do the kind of lung damage that was earlier thought.

Even the military has been having big problems with Spice.

No one has ever overdosed on cannabis (marijuana) and if used alone there is no reason why anyone would end up in the emergency room.

Cannabis does not cause violent behavior or agitation and with moderate use is not addictive.

This can't be said about tobacco and alcohol yet those are sold every day to anyone of legal age. They both are harmful substances that can cause death if abused.

More to Come

Synthetic marijuana will continue to evolve, to stay one step ahead of the law. People will continue to smoke unknown chemicals that may or may not result in a seizure or bizarre hallucination, endangering their lives and others in turn, all because what they really want to smoke is illegal.

Maybe we should look at why cannabis is illegal and who benefits from that? There are many things you have not been told about. It has medicinal properties which show incredible promise. At this point, I would be interested to see evidence that it does not kill cancer as even the National Cancer Institute has said it has antitumor properties.

There is much, much more to come. It is time the people let the emperor know he has no clothes.

EVALUATING THE AUTHOR'S ARGUMENTS:

Viewpoint author Diane Kearns-Carlstrom argues that users of synthetic marijuana would prefer to smoke natural marijuana. Given the dangers of synthetic marijuana, do you think that natural marijuana should be legalized for recreational use? Why or why not? Support your answer with evidence from this text.

High Society: Drugs Don't Liberate— Quite the Opposite

Peter Hitchens

> *"We should have laws against cannabis, and . . . they should be enforced."*

Marijuana is a dangerous drug that can cause irreversible damage to the mind and should never be legalized, argues Peter Hitchens in the following viewpoint. Many cannabis users are too young to understand the harm that they might inflict on themselves and their families, he contends. Moreover, Hitchens maintains that England's lax drug laws enable marijuana use and fail to properly punish those found in possession of the drug. In his view, nations that tolerate drugs like marijuana are simply inviting societal numbness, sloth, breakdown, and failure. Hitchens is a columnist for the *Mail on Sunday*, a British newspaper. He is also the author of *The War We Never Fought: The British Establishment's Surrender to Drugs*.

AS YOU READ, CONSIDER THE FOLLOWING QUESTIONS:
1. What was the nature of the "demonstration" against Hitchens, as he relates?
2. In the author's view, why is the use of cannabis a "gift for authority"?
3. According to Hitchens, why is England quiet about its lax enforcement of drug laws?

How thrilling it is when someone finally stages a demonstration against you. All right, it was a very small protest (one person), and it was in Southampton on a wet Sunday morning. But it was all mine. Stretched by the roadside was a dank bedsheet bearing the words 'Peter Hitchens is a hypocritical racist alcoholic. Spread your bile elsewhere. No one cares what you have to say.' I don't accept this as entirely accurate, but, under the circumstances, why quibble? Also, it made me think.

Standing beside it, smirking, was a person in a woolly hat and sunglasses. He had a striking pallor, the sort you might get from spending many months in a basement with a computer, converting sugary drinks into lard. What had provoked this manifestation of political rage and personal scorn? After a brief and unsatisfactory conversation, in which our minds did not meet, I grasped that the problem was my view that we should have laws against cannabis, and that they should be enforced. My critic thinks that this drug is a moral cause. For him, the freedom to take it ranks alongside the freedoms of speech, thought and assembly. There are many like him and a surprising number are conservatives, or write for conservative publications.

This seems to me to be plain wrong, in many ways. Cannabis users may think they are islands of joy. But they often inflict dreadful harm on others, especially their own families. Many of them are far too young to know what they are doing, endangering not just their intelligence and their schooling, but perhaps their very sanity. Those who doubt this should reflect on the painful fate of Henry Cockburn, son of Patrick, so movingly recorded in their book *Henry's Demons*.

I had assumed that most thoughtful people would see that a properly enforced law would be the best weapon against the ghastly peer-pressure which persuades suggestible schoolchildren to risk the capricious, irreversible danger to their mental health which cannabis threatens. If such a law was inconvenient for a few pleasure-seekers, then surely they could not be so selfish as to sacrifice the wellbeing of other people's children for their own delight? Oh yes, they could. Not long afterwards, I met a similar fury from a rather different quarter. This time my assailant was Sam Bowman, policy director of the Adam Smith Institute. Accusing me of authoritarianism, he asserted: 'As an adult, I should be able to stick whatever I damn well like into my body. Provided that I am aware of the risks, nobody is better placed to make my personal cost/benefit calculation for any given action.'

Could it really be that dope and liberty were allies? No. Legalised drugs mean a society in which the mind is dead and in which all kinds of wickedness, sloth and failure prosper. The mass use of drugs such as cannabis is a gift for authority, which must be secretly delighted by the passive acquiescence which results.

Aldous Huxley, a far more accurate prophet than George Orwell, saw it coming in *Brave New World*, a dystopia where the loins were free and the mind was enslaved. He feared above all things that people could be made to love and enjoy their own servitude. Vital to this was 'soma', his imaginary happiness drug, which had 'all the advantages of Christianity and alcohol; none of their defects . . . take a holiday from reality whenever you like and come back without so much as a headache or a mythology'.

Soma is already appearing in our midst, without protest or alarm. The current mass prescription of 'antidepressants' and 'tranquillisers', along with the feeding of powerful mind-altering pills to children alleged to suffer from ADHD, looks to me like the rapid fulfilment of this prophecy. A numbed nation deals with economic decline, unemployment, family breakdown, illiteracy and bad schools, not by reforming these ills, but by doping their victims so that they can more easily endure these things.

FAST FACT

The US Office of National Drug Policy contends that marijuana use is associated with respiratory and mental illness, impaired immune function, and difficulty in thinking and problem solving.

What if a way could be found to allow the commercial sale of cannabis too? That development is also far closer than most people think. This country pretends to have stern anti-drug laws, and some people (notably the otherwise astute Sir Simon Jenkins) take this claim at face value. But it does not take much study to find that cannabis is at least as decriminalised in this country as it is Amsterdam. We just don't advertise our laxity, partly because older voters are not ready for the truth, partly because we are bound by international treaties to maintain at least the semblance of a law against it.

How is it that, in a country where drugs are supposedly illegal—where 'evil dealers' are endlessly denounced—that drugs are so common and that little or nothing happens to those who are caught in possession of them? How did the 'cannabis warning', a gesture without force or penalty, unsanctioned by Parliament, become the preferred response of the police to the crime of possession? How can Pete Doherty drop illegal drugs on the floor of a courthouse, be caught by a security guard and yet walk free from the building, if we are—as we are so often told—running a regime of stern prohibition?

The answer is that the official version of events is simply false. Since a momentous Cabinet meeting in February 1970, there has been no 'war on drugs' in this country, only the official pretence of one. I beg my fellow commentators, columnists and pundits: please do not take seriously any claims that our drug problems stem from zealous enforcement of cruel laws, or you might find me camping outside your front door in a woolly hat, denouncing you and proclaiming your sins on a bedsheet.

EVALUATING THE AUTHOR'S ARGUMENTS:

How would you describe the tone of Peter Hitchens's viewpoint? In your opinion, does his tone strengthen his argument or detract from it? Explain.

Facts About Synthetic Drugs

Editor's note: These facts can be used in reports to add credibility when making important points or claims.

Synthetic Cannabis/Marijuana:
- Also known as K2, Spice, Black Mamba, Ocean Breeze, Dragon, Bombay, and other street names. Often sold as baggies or containers of crushed herbs sprayed with chemicals that mimic ingredients in cannabis and labeled as herbal incense or potpourri.
- The effects of synthetic cannabis include: elevated mood, relaxation, and altered perceptions. Some users report adverse effects such as extreme anxiety, paranoia, hallucinations, and addiction. Severe effects include heart problems, panic attacks, seizures, and strokes.
- Natural cannabis contains THC as well as cannabidiol (CBD), which have anticonvulsive and antipsychotic properties. The absence of CBD in synthetic cannabis increases the likelihood of psychotic symptoms and seizures.
- According to the Substance Abuse and Mental Health Services Administration, there were 11,406 emergency department visits involving synthetic cannabis in 2010. In 2011 emergency department visits involving the same product had increase two and a half times to 28,531.

Synthetic Cathinones (Mephedrone, etc.):
- Also known as bath salts and plant food, as well as by product names such as Ivory Wave, Vanilla Sky, Bliss, Blue Silk, Cosmic Wave, Ocean, Cloud Nine, and other street names. Often sold as a crystalline white powder in small baggies marked "not for human consumption."
- The effects of mephedrone are: euphoria, increased energy, and heightened sociability and sex drive. Some users report paranoia, agitation, delirium, and insomnia. Serious adverse effects include violent behavior, high blood pressure, psychosis, heart attack, brain damage, and stroke.

MDMA (Ecstasy or Molly)

- Molly (short for "molecular") refers to the pure crystalline powder form of MDMA and is usually sold in capsules.
- The effects of MDMA are: euphoria, increased energy, sensory distortions, emotional warmth, and empathy toward others. Negative physical effects can include nausea, chills and sweating, blurred vision, muscular tension, and involuntary teeth clenching. In the days and weeks following dosage, users may experience confusion, depression, anxiety, and insomnia.
- In high doses, MDMA can cause hyperthermia (a sharp increase in body temperature) which can, in rare cases, lead to liver, kidney, and heart failure and even death.

Ketamine

- Ketamine, also known as Special K, is a pain reliever used mostly in veterinary practices.
- The effects of ketamine include: distorted visual and sound perceptions and feelings of detachment from one's surroundings and self. Higher doses can result in dreamlike states, hallucinations, delirium, and amnesia. Adverse effects include impaired motor function, high blood pressure, urinary tract system damage, and potentially fatal respiratory problems.
- Ketamine users can develop signs of tolerance, dependence, and cravings for the drug.

According to the US Office of National Drug Control Policy:

- Fifty-one new synthetic cannabinoids were identified in 2012, compared with just two in 2009.
- Thirty-one new synthetic cathinones were identified in 2012, compared with just four in 2009.
- Seventy-six other synthetic compounds were identified in 2012, bringing the total number of new synthetic substances discovered that year to 158.
- One out of nine US high school seniors reported using synthetic marijuana in the past year, making it the second most frequently used illegal drug among this age group after natural marijuana.
- Synthetic marijuana is the third most widely used substance after natural marijuana and inhalants among US 8th graders.

According to the National Institute on Drug Abuse

- In 2012, 13 percent of 8th graders, 30 percent of 10th graders, and 40 percent of 12th graders reported using any illegal substance.
- In 2012, 4.4 percent of 8th graders, 8.8 percent of 10th graders, and 11.3 percent of 12th graders used synthetic marijuana. In contrast, 11 percent of 8th graders, 28 percent of 10th graders, and 36 percent of 12th graders used natural marijuana.
- In 2012 nearly twice as many male senior high school students reported use of synthetic marijuana as did females in the same age group.
- In 2012, 0.8 percent of 8th graders, 0.6 percent of 10th graders, and 1.3 percent of 12th graders used synthetic cathinones (bath salts).
- Bath salts are marketed as cheap substitutes for cocaine or Ecstasy. They raise dopamine levels in the brain in the same manner that cocaine does but are at least ten times more potent than cocaine.
- Bath salts can cause a syndrome known as "excited delirium"; symptoms can include dehydration, breakdown of skeletal muscle tissue, and kidney failure.
- The 2012 prevalence rate for Ecstasy use was 1.1 percent among 8th graders, 3 percent among 10th graders, and 3.8 percent among 12th graders.
- Molly capsules frequently contain substances other than MDMA, including ephedrine or methamphetamine (stimulants), dextromethorphan (a cough suppressant), ketamine, cocaine, caffeine, or synthetic cathinones (bath salts). Mixing such substances can be particularly dangerous and lead to adverse health effects.
- In 2009, 1 percent of 8th graders, 1.3 percent of 10th graders, and 1.7 percent of high school seniors reported using ketamine. By 2012, less than one percent of 8th graders and 10th graders and 1.5 percent of 12th graders reported ketamine use.

Organizations to Contact

The editors have compiled the following list of organizations concerned with the issues debated in this book. The descriptions are derived from materials provided by the organizations. All have publications or information available for interested readers. The list was compiled on the date of publication of the present volume; the information provided here may change. Be aware that many organizations take several weeks or longer to respond to inquiries, so allow as much time as possible for the receipt of requested materials.

Drug Free America Foundation (DFAF)
5999 Central Ave., Ste. 301
Saint Petersburg, FL 33710
(727) 828-0211
fax: (727) 828-0212
website: www.dfaf.org

The DFAF is a nongovernmental drug prevention and policy organization committed to developing, promoting, and sustaining global strategies, policies, and laws that will reduce illegal drug use, drug addiction, and drug-related injuries and deaths. Its reference collection contains more than twenty-one hundred books and other media chronicling the rise of the drug culture and current drug policy issues. It favors the war on drugs, and its website contains many articles defending current policy, including student drug testing.

Erowid
PO Box 1116
Grass Valley, CA 95945
e-mail: sage@erowid.org
website: www.erowid.org

Erowid is a member-supported organization whose mission is to provide access to reliable information about psychoactive plants, chemicals, and related issues. It works with academic, medical, and experiential experts to develop and publish new resources, as well as to improve and increase access to already existing resources. The organization's website provides information on hundreds of psychoactive substances, including effects, legal status, and health considerations. Of particular note are the Experience Vaults, which contain close to one hundred thousand first-hand descriptions of psychoactive drug use. Erowid also provides links to online books about psychoactive drugs and publishes the newsletter *Erowid Extracts* twice a year.

Independent Scientific Committee on Drugs (ISCD)
Centre for Crime and Justice Studies
2 Langley Lane
London SW8 1GB
UK
e-mail: info@drugscience.org.uk
website: www.drugscience.org.uk

The ISCD is the leading independent scientific body on the harms and benefits of both illegal and controlled drugs in the United Kingdom. Its drug scientists work together to ensure that the public can access clear, evidence-based information on drugs without interference from political or commercial interests. The organization addresses issues surrounding drug harms and benefits, regulation and education, prevention, treatment, and recovery. Its website offers detailed information on numerous drugs (both legal and illegal), a newsletter, links to additional resources on the Internet, and links to follow ISCD chairman David Nutt on Facebook and Twitter.

Integral Recovery
PO Box 146
Teasdale, UT 84773
(435) 691-1193
e-mail: johndupuy@gmail.com
website: www.integralrecovery.com

Integral Recovery is an addiction recovery program founded by John Dupuy that attempts to address all relevant aspects of body, mind, heart, and spirit to achieve recovery from substance addiction and enhanced health and well-being. Its website offers articles, audio and video material on addiction recovery, as well as a blog by Dupuy. Consultation and coaching services are available, as well as recommendations for other programs to help addicts and their families.

International Centre for Science in Drug Policy (ICSDP)
608–1081 Burrard St.
Vancouver, BC V6Z 1Y6
Canada
e-mail: info@icsdp.org
website: www.icsdp.org

The ICSDP is an international network of scientists, academics, and health practitioners committed to improving the health and safety of communities and individuals affected by illicit drugs. The center includes leading experts from around the world who have come together in an effort to inform drug policies with the best available scientific evidence. The organization's website offers research reports and summaries, a blog, press releases, an e-mail newsletter and e-alerts, as well as links to follow the ICSDP's work through Facebook and Twitter.

Law Enforcement Against Prohibition (LEAP)
121 Mystic Ave., Stes. 7–9
Medford, MA 02155
(781) 393-6985
fax: (781) 393-2964
e-mail: info@leap.cc
website: www.leap.cc

LEAP is a nonprofit educational organization founded by police officers. Its mission is to reduce the multitude of unintended harmful consequences resulting from fighting the war on drugs. Its website contains many articles and multimedia presentations explaining why it believes legalizing drugs would be a more effective way of reducing the crime, disease, and addiction drugs cause. Publications offered on the LEAP website include *End Prohibition Now!, Why I Want All Drugs Legalized,* and *Ending the Drug War: A Dream Deferred.* Other offerings include videos, a blog, the *LEAP Newsletter,* and links to LEAP feeds on Facebook, Twitter, YouTube, and Myspace.

Multidisciplinary Association for Psychedelic Studies (MAPS)
309 Cedar St. #2323
Santa Cruz, CA 95060
(831) 429-6362
fax: (831) 429-6370
e-mail: aslonaps@maps.org
website: http://maps.org

MAPS is a nonprofit research and educational organization that aims to educate the public about the risks and benefits of mind-altering drugs and to develop those substances into prescription medicines. Its website offers a vast array of information, including reports on the use of MDMA for the treatment of post-traumatic stress disorder, research papers, free literature, and audio and video material. An e-mail newsletter is available, as well as the triannual *MAPS Bulletin*, the entire archives of which are available on the website. MAPS also hosts a moderated discussion forum via e-mail.

**National Center on Addiction and
Substance Abuse (CASA Columbia)**
633 Third Ave., 19th Fl.
New York, NY 10017-6706
(212) 841-5200
website: www.casacolumbia.org

CASAColumbia is a private, nonprofit organization that works to educate the public about the hazards of chemical dependency. The organization supports treatment as the best way to reduce chemical dependency and produces numerous publications describing the harmful effects of drug addiction and effective ways to address the problem of substance abuse. Books published by CASAColumbia include *HIGH SOCIETY: How Substance Abuse Ravages America and What to Do About It* and *How to Raise a Drug-Free Kid: The Straight Dope for Parents.* Its website also features videos and the quarterly *CASA Inside* newsletter.

National Institute on Drug Abuse (NIDA)
Office of Science Policy and Communications
Public Information and Liaison Branch
6001 Executive Blvd., Rm. 5213, MSC 9561

Bethesda, MD 20892-9561
(301) 443-1124
e-mail: information@nida.nih.gov
website: www.drugabuse.gov

NIDA is one of the National Institutes of Health, a component of the US Department of Health and Human Services. NIDA supports and conducts research on drug abuse to improve addiction prevention, treatment, and policy efforts. It is dedicated to understanding how drugs of abuse affect the brain and behavior, and it works to rapidly disseminate new information to policy makers, drug abuse counselors, and the general public. It publishes the *NIDA Notes* and *What's New at NIDA?* newsletters as well as "DrugFacts," summarizing key information on different psychoactive substances. The website also offers videos, podcasts, e-books, and a section on related topics, such as addiction science, drug testing, and trends and statistics. Of particular note is the "NIDA for Teens" section (http://teens.drugabuse.gov).

Office of National Drug Control Policy (ONDCP)
Drug Policy Information Clearinghouse
PO Box 6000
Rockville, MD 20849-6000
(800) 666-3332
fax: (301) 519-5212
e-mail: ondcp@ncjrs.org
website: www.whitehouse.gov/ondcp

The ONDCP is responsible for formulating the US government's national drug strategy as well as coordinating the federal agencies responsible for stopping drug trafficking. It has launched drug prevention programs, including the National Youth Anti-Drug Media Campaign and Above the Influence. The ONDCP's website features fact sheets, such as "Synthetic Drugs," "Alternatives to Incarceration," and "A Medical Approach to Drug Prevention," as well as a blog, news releases, and information on treatment and recovery.

The Partnership at Drugfree.org
405 Lexington Ave., Ste. 1601
New York, NY 10174

(212) 922-1560
website: www.drugfree.org

The Partnership at Drugfree.org, previously known as the Partnership for a Drug-Free America, is a nonprofit organization that utilizes the media to reduce demand for illicit drugs in America. Best known for its national antidrug advertising campaigns, the partnership works to educate children about the dangers of drugs and to prevent drug use among youths. It produces the *Partnership Newsletter*, annual reports, and monthly press releases about current events with which the partnership is involved. Also available at its website is a drug guide to commonly abused drugs—including bath salts, ketamine, Molly, and other synthetic drugs—and sections on prevention, intervention, treatment, and recovery.

US Drug Enforcement Administration (DEA)
Office of Diversion Control
8701 Morrissette Dr.
Springfield, VA 22152
(202) 307-1000
website: www.justice.gov/dea

The DEA is the federal agency charged with enforcing the nation's drug laws and regulations. It coordinates the activities of federal, state, and local agencies and works with foreign governments to reduce the availability of illicit drugs in the United States. The DEA publishes the biannual *Microgram Journal* and the monthly *Microgram Bulletins*. Numerous DEA publications are available on its website, including *Drugs of Abuse, Get It Straight: The Facts About Drugs Student Guide,* and *Speaking Out Against Drug Legalization*. Drug fact sheets, videos, and a section specifically for teens can also be found on its website (www. justthinktwice.com).

US Substance Abuse and Mental Health Services Administration (SAMHSA)
1 Choke Cherry Rd.
Rockville, MD 20857
(877) 726-4727
fax: (240) 221-4292
e-mail: samhsainfo@samhsa.hhs.gov
website: www.samhsa.gov

The mission of SAMHSA is to reduce the impact of substance abuse and mental illness on America's communities. It aims to help create communities where individuals, families, schools, faith-based organizations, and workplaces take action to promote emotional health and reduce the likelihood of mental illness, substance abuse, and suicide. Publications available on its website include *Results from the 2011 National Survey on Drug Use and Health (NSDUH)* as well as brochures and fact sheets on MDMA, bath salts, ketamine, PCP, and numerous other abused drugs.

For Further Reading

Books

Caulkins, Jonathan P. et al. *Marijuana Legalization: What Everyone Needs to Know.* New York: Oxford University Press, 2012. In this nonpartisan book, public policy experts examine the risks and benefits of marijuana legalization.

Gerald, Michael C. *The Drug Book: From Arsenic to Xanax, 250 Milestones in the History of Drugs.* New York: Sterling, 2013. From ancient herbs to cutting-edge chemicals, this text looks at hundreds of the most important moments in the development of life-altering, lifesaving, and sometimes life-endangering pharmaceuticals.

Get Smart About Synthetic Drugs (A Hazelden Quick Guide). E-book. Center City, MN: Hazelden, 2013. Expert resources and information are combined in a book that examines the history of synthetic drug use and abuse as well as the health effects of these drugs and intervention and effective treatment methods for addicts.

Koellhoffer, Tara. *Ecstasy and Other Club Drugs.* New York: Chelsea House, 2008. This Junior Drug Awareness book explains the origins and effects of MDMA (Ecstasy) and other designer club drugs.

Lewis, Marc. *Memoirs of an Addicted Brain: A Neuroscientist Examines His Former Life on Drugs.* New York: Public Affairs, 2013. As a bullied fifteen-year-old, Lewis escaped reality by drinking alcohol and smoking marijuana. Later he used LSD, methamphetamines, and other drugs, turning to a life of crime to support his addictions. He eventually recovered and became a researcher in psychology and neuroscience. In this book, he recounts his own journey through addiction to tell the universal story of addictions of every kind.

Nutt, David. *Drugs Without the Hot Air: Minimizing the Harms of Legal and Illegal Drugs.* Cambridge, England: UIT Cambridge, 2012. The author examines how various pharmaceutical substances affect the body and the mind, and he invites people to make rational decisions about drugs based on objective evidence rather than sensationalism.

Parks, Peggy J. *Bath Salts and Other Synthetic Drugs.* San Diego: Reference Point, 2013. The author outlines the dangers of bath salts and similar substances, exploring possibilities for regulating these chemicals and for preventing synthetic drug abuse.

Taylor, Russ. *Bath Salts: An Inside Look at the Synthetic Drug Phenomenon.* Seattle: CreateSpace Independent Publishing Platform, 2012. A brief booklet that examines the truth behind designer drugs and synthetic substances camouflaged as household products.

Periodicals and Internet Sources

Barshad, Amos and Annie Ferrer, "Salts Tripping: The Latest Very-Bad-for-You Designer Drug Has Nothing to Do with the Stuff that Goes in a Tub," *New York*, February 11, 2011.

"'Bath Salts' Stimulant Could Be More Addictive than Meth," *Medical News Today*, July 12, 2013.

Breese, Chris. "The Party's Over: How Drug Use Ruined My Life," *Nottingham Evening Post*, June 6, 2013.

Brown, Andrew M. "Psychedelic Revival: Mind-Bending Drugs Are Making a Comeback—In the Field of Psychiatry," *Spectator*, August 18, 2012.

Campbell, Becky. "Fake Drugs, Real Consequences," *Johnson City Press*, February 4, 2012. www.johnsoncitypress.com/article/98058.

Carraway, Nick. "The Addictive Yet Deadly Spice (Military Deal with New Drugs)," *Free Republic*, November 25, 2011. www.free republic.com/focus/f-chat/2812293/posts.

Dean, Dave. "Can MDMA Cure PTSD?" Vice.com, April 2013. www.vice.com/read/can-mdma-cure-ptsd.

Doward, Jamie and Silvia Suarez Jiminez. "Ecstasy Is Back in Clubs as Newly Potent Drug Is Taken with 'Legal Highs,'" *The Observer*, November 19, 2011. www.theguardian.com/society/2011/nov/20/ecstasy-returns-to-clubs.

Dwoskin, Elizabeth. "Global Economics: To Stop Designer Drugs, an Early Warning System Is Born," *Bloomberg Businessweek*, April 11, 2013.

Frank, Howard. "Popular Club Drug Replaced by a More Toxic One: Cloud Nine," *Pocono Record* (Stroudsburg, PA), January 18, 2012. www.poconorecord.com/apps/pbcs.dll/article?AID =/20120118/NEWS/201180322/-l/rss38.

Gardner, Amanda. "Hallucinogens Legally Sold as 'Bath Salts' a New Threat," *Consumer Health News*, February 4, 2011.

Gray, Keven. "A Higher Powder," *Details*, August 2010.

Keim, Brandon. "Chemists Outrun Laws in War on Synthetic Drugs," *Wired*, May 30, 2012. www.wired.com/wiredscience/2012/05 /synthetic-drug-war/.

Lawal, Riki. "Drug War Takes Aim at Synthetic Marijuana," *Washington Post*, April 25, 2013.

Lewis, Alana. "'Frankenstein' Drug Screws the Mind Up," *Europe Intelligence Wire*, September 5, 2012.

Marder, Jenny. "Bath Salts: The Drug That Never Lets Go," *PBS Newshour*, September 20, 2012. www.pbs.org/newshour/multi media/bath-salts/.

Matthews, Meredith M. "Bitter Pill: Ecstasy Is a Club You Don't Want to Join," *Current Health Teens*, March 2010.

McKie, Robin. "Ecstasy Does Not Wreck the Mind, Study Says," *The Observer*, February 19, 2011. www.theguardian.com/society /2011/feb/19/ecstasy-harm-brain-new-study.

Nutt, David. "The Miami Face-Eating Case Should Not Stampede US into a 'Bath Salts' Ban," *The Guardian*, May 31, 2012. www .guardian.co.uk/commentisfree/2012/may/31/miami-face-eating -case-bath-salts-ban.

O'Neill, Tony. "The Truth Behind the Bath Salt 'Epidemic,'" *The Fix*, June 17, 2012. www.thefix.com/content/bath-salt-scare -10084?page=all.

Ot'alora, Marcela. "Possibilities for Growth: Working with Trauma," *Treating PTSD with MDMA-Assisted Psychotherapy*, 2012. www .mdmaptsd.org/testimonials/65-possibilities-for-growth.html.

Park, Madison. "New Zealand: Prove Recreational Drug Is Safe, Then You Can Sell." www.cnn.com, July 11, 2013.

Phelan, Benjamin. "Our Chemical Romance," *Details*, May 2012.

Rose, Joel. "Fake Pot Is a Real Problem for Regulators." www.npr
.com, July 12, 2012.

Sarah, Naomi. "Dangers of Smoking Spice," Buzzle.com, May
30, 2012. www.buzzle.com/articles/dangers-of-smoking-spice
.html.

Slater, Lauren. "A Kaleidoscope at the End of the Tunnel," *New York
Times Magazine*, April 22, 2012.

Smith, Mikelle D. "Spice: A Temporary High for a Permanent
Change: How It Affects Your Body and Your Navy Career," *All
Hands*, September 2011.

"Study of Ketamine May Lead to Drug Offering Rapid Relief from
Depression," *Mental Health Weekly*, October 22, 2012.

Szalavitz, Maia. "Ecstasy as Therapy: Have Some of Its Negative
Effects Been Overblown?" *Time*, February 18, 2011. http://health
land.time.com/2011/02/18/ecstasy-as-therapy-have-some-of-its
-negative-effects-been-overblown/.

Szalavitz, Maia. "Exaggerating the Risk of Drugs Harms Us All,"
The Fix, July 1, 2013. www.thefix.com/content/harm-benefits-drug
-war-abstinence8509.

Van Pelt, Jennifer. "Synthetic Drugs—Fake Substances, Real
Dangers," *Social Work Today*, July/August 2012. www.social
worktoday.com/archive/070212p12.shtml.

Websites

Drug Free America Foundation, Inc (www.dfaf.org). This website
includes a link to the Otto and Connie Moulton Library for Drug
Prevention, a reference collection that contains more than 2,100
books and other media chronicling the rise of the drug culture and
current drug policy issues. In addition, a "Q&A" tab offers information on drug testing, overcoming addiction, and international
drug policy.

Drug Policy Alliance (www.drugpolicy.org). This website features
a "Publications and Resources" section that includes links to an
online resource library with more than fifteen thousand documents
and videos. Fact Sheets, drug war statistics, drug policy updates,
reports, and the booklet *Safety First: A Reality- Based Approach to*

Teens and Drugs are among the materials available through links at this reform-minded organization's home page.

White House Office of National Drug Control Policy (www .whitehouse.gov/ondcp). At this website's "Issues" link, several informative reports and fact sheets are available, including "Synthetic Drugs," "Lifting the Stigma of Addiction," "Drug-Endangered Children," and "Alternatives to Incarceration."

Index

Food and Drug Administration, US (FDA), 65, 67

G
GAO (US Government Accountability Office), 29
Glatter, Robert, 33
Globe and Mail (newspaper), 107
Government Accountability Office, US (GAO), 29
Grant, Igor, 73
Guardian (newspaper), 44

H
Halpern, John, 35–36
Harvey, Fiona, 43
Hirsch, Neil, 71
Hitchens, Peter, 109
Holub, Gary, 58
Huffman, John W., 104
Huxley, Aldous, 111

I
Institute of Medicine (IOM), 67–68
Internet, international drug trade and, 46
Iversen, Leslie, 20

J
Janda, Kim, 99, 100, 101–102
Johnson, Alan, 19
Join Together, 12
Journal of Psychopharmacology, 55

K
K2. *See* Cannabinoids, synthetic recreational
Kearns-Carlstrom, Diane, 103
Kendall, Perry, 56
Ketamine (Special K), 32, 40, 45
overall harm score of, *28*
Khat, 8, 19, 94
overall harm score of, *28*
Kleber, Herbert, 72–73, 74
Klimax. *See* Cannabinoids, synthetic
Köllisch, Anton, 57
Kush. *See* Cannabinoids, synthetic
Kushner, Logan, 106

L
Lallanilla, Marc, 21
Laurance, Jeremy, 18
Lee, Joseph, 12
Lembke, Traci, 86
Leonhart, Michele M., 86
Los Angeles Times (newspaper), 74

M
Macrae, Fiona, 59
Madonna, *35*
Marijuana
adverse health effects of, 111
legalization of, would curb abuse of synthetic marijuana, 103–108
overall harm score of, *28*
past-year use/perceived risk of, among high school seniors, *24, 68*

National Institute on Drug Abuse (NIDA), 22
  on long-lasting effects of MDMA, 60
National Post (newspaper), 55
National Survey on Drug Use and Health, 40, 51
Nichols, Brian, 44
NIDA (National Institute on Drug Abuse), 22
Nutt, David, 60

O

Obama, Barack, 23, 77, 78–79
Ocean Breeze. *See* Cannabinoids, synthetic recreational
Office of National Drug Control Policy (ONDCP), 76, 111
Opinion polls. *See* Surveys

P

Pacey, Ingrid, 55, 57, 58
Payne, Rusty, 33
Pemberton, Max, 91
Plant food. *See* Cathinones, synthetic; Mephedrone
Poison Control Centers, calls related to synthetic drugs, *15*
Polls. *See* Surveys
Popular culture, MDMA promoted in, 33–34
Post-traumatic stress disorder (PTSD), 36
  MDMA is effective in treatment of, 54–58

percentage of subjects qualifying for diagnosis and, *57*
  prevalence of diagnosis, 56
Pressfield, Steven, 83
Prison population, US, before *vs.* after start of war on drugs, *82*
Project Synergy, 85–86
Psychoactive Substances Bill (New Zealand, 2013), 9–10
PTSD. *See* Post-traumatic stress disorder
Pure Food and Drug Act (1906), 66

R

Reducing the Illicit U.S. Demand for Drugs (United States Senate Caucus on International Narcotics), 81
Reefer Madness (film), 27, *27*

S

Sabet, Kevin, 82–83
Scott, Rick, 104
Scripps Research Institute, 97
The Scripps Research Institute (TSRI), 98
Sekaran, Sharda, 26
Shapiro, Harry, 51–52
Smith, Nicholas, 19
Soda, Christopher, 80
Special K. *See* Ketamine
Spice, *49*
Spice
  See also Cannabinoids, synthetic recreational

Picture Credits